I JUST WANT TO SEE TREES

I JUST WANT TO SEE TREES

— A Journey Through PTSD —
(Post Traumatic Stress Disorder)

MARC RACITI

Illustration design by Sonja Raciti
Cover and Book design by JONES MEDIA PUBLISHING
www.YourBookBlueprint.com

ISBN 978-0-9973408-2-2 PAPERBACK

This book is dedicated to the brave men and women who paid the ultimate sacrifice and never returned home. To those who did come home that are lost, broken and cannot see trees. For my brothers and sisters in arms.

My wife Sonja who has been my anchor through out this journey. Sam for being there for me in my darkest hour. David and the Wolf hound Medics for being a great influence in my book. Dr. CC Woo AKA MM who has been my brother, mentor, and friend all these years. Joel and Clint for mentoring, teaching and for being there when the chips were down. Lance for cracking me up all these years. My Father in-law Norman Hershfield for final editing of my book.

CONTENTS

PREFACE

"Losing your way on a journey is unfortunate. But, losing your-
reason for the journey is a fate more cruel." ~ H.G. Wells

HOW DOES ONE GET LOST? The answer is more complex than you can imagine. In combat, there are casualties and fatalities, so it's obvious when a loved one is lost. It's tangible, quantifiable, and there are procedures in place. The military notifies the soldier's spouse and family members, giving them a chance to mourn and process their loss. Then, there is a funeral and eventually, closure. This protocol is in place to ease the pain of the surviving families.

What about the surviving soldiers? How do they get lost and what are the consequences? There are multiple ways this happens. Some soldiers come home and exit the military because their enlistment is up and they do not choose to reenlist. Others are lost due to medical or administrative reasons. Sometimes returning soldiers are asked to leave as a result of bad behavior, or inferior performance.

And, last and certainly most tragically, we lose the soldiers who never returned home because they felt suicide was the best way to escape the horrors of Post Traumatic Stress Disorder (PTSD). The Armed forces, veterans, and military retirees make around 7% of the entire American population (with vets being the largest population), yet they the highest suicide rate of any subgroup in our country.

The problem is that PTSD often does not manifest until months after one is back from a deployment. Soldiers leave the military in haste before their symptoms begin to appear and then find themselves without any PTSD support in the civilian world. In these cases, they start developing bad behaviors, rapidly going through their savings and sometimes tempting fate with risky behavior, such as taking drugs or drinking to excess, ultimately resulting in a loss in the form of incarceration or death.

Sonja and I wrote this book to share our own personal journey through the most difficult and painful part of our lives. We want to share our experiences with the hope that our small victories will offer hope to those who have had or are currently struggling with PTSD.

The intent is to help others make sense of this disorder and learn to live with it. We say "live with it" because, as we will illustrate throughout the book, PTSD never quite goes away. By bringing this syndrome to the forefront, we hope to offer a better understanding of the impact PTSD has on us and our nation.

For every one person who gets help, there are 10 who choose to live with it and avoid treatment. Living with PTSD causes many people to have serious interpersonal relationship issues as well as chronic depression. We suffer countless sleepless nights as a result of being woken up by the ghosts of our past. I have gone fortunately from this very dark and self-destructive phase to a healing phase. I say healing because I think that once you have PTSD and get help, you begin to heal—very slowly—but healing is not the same as being cured. PTSD is a chronic condition and medication only manages part of it. Therapy manages the rest.

Writing this book has given us direction and purpose. Through our story we wish to offer our support to those who have crossed the abyss, and, for those who are still in the midst of crossing, we will be here on the other side to greet you.

Some of the names in this book have been changed in order to protect the privacy of others.

INTRODUCTION

THIS STORY IS ABOUT MY journey, from the very first time I realized there was a problem, to the moment I found the courage to get well. It was not an easy thing to accomplish, but somehow I managed to cross this abyss that defines my struggle and journey. My hope is that I will be able to inspire others to want to get well, and to help those who continue to suffer and may never get completely well.

The concept is simple: It's about paying it forward – to help veterans and others with PTSD make it across the abyss. Once on the healing side, my wish is that they, in turn, will start helping others who are lost, and thus establish a culture of understanding and compassion for our PTSD population.

When our service members returned from Vietnam, very little effort was put into finding ways to treat or understand what was known at the time as "Gross Stress Reaction." It was a very different time, and public support was not with the veterans or an unpopular war. Even today, those veterans are still fighting with the Veterans Administration for compensation—something that was owed to them when they started having symptoms. Instead, their claims were swept under a rug of indifference and a political, dissociative climate. Their PTSD symptoms were chalked up to drug abuse and poor conduct. PTSD was not even included in the Diagnostic and Statistical Manual of Mental Disorders III until 1980.

Today, PTSD is taken seriously, partially due to the tragic military installation shootings that took place at Fort Hood, Texas and the Navy Shipyard, Washington D.C. Negative press can be very persuasive on big government. This was again exemplified in 2014 by the events at the Veterans Affairs Hospital in Phoenix, Arizona, where patients were ignored and some even died while waiting to be treated for PTSD. This neglect leading to multiple deaths brought national attention to the VA, which, subsequently, partially cleaned up its act.

On a less cynical note, I can say that our government and military have worked hard to establish a culture of care by screening our returning service members for anxiety and depression, and offering counseling and help both at the military clinics and the Soldier Readiness Centers.

But, even with all that attention, there is still a lot about PTSD that we as a society do not know or understand. With this book I hope to shed some light and help you understand this complex disease through the eyes of a clinician and soldier who suffers from PTSD. Writing this book has been very challenging for me because it forced me to revisit all my feelings and draw upon suppressed memories of events the way I remember them. The stories may not always be accurate, but this is how I recall them.

Adding to the difficulty of the process, is the fact that the very essence of the disease is avoidance, so writing about very personal, and, often painful, memories was challenging. I had to take a lot of breaks, and at times I would not write a word for months. Eventually, though, I would start again, because ultimately the goal was to complete the book and face my own fears, including reliving my darkest hour where I found myself standing in front of a tree, intending to kill myself.

Behind me lies a wide trail of severed relationships many of which are beyond repair. I look back sometimes in shame and wonder if I could have done this any other way, but I find solace knowing that somehow, through it all, I managed to cross the abyss. The person who emerged from that nightmare has PTSD and has learned to live with it.

On the other hand, ahead of me there is rebuilding my life and bridging the gap left behind in the hearts of my loved ones. I am taking time to smell the roses and to simply love life and all that it has in store for me. I see myself laughing and smiling more often, slowly getting back on track and becoming the man I was intended to become. Now going to see a counselor is merely a tune-up visit. Daily medication keeps me happy, with low anxiety and depression levels. I suppose I will have to manage PTSD throughout my life, but I can also say that, for the most part, my life has improved tremendously. I am slowly finding all the parts of me that are replenishing the voids left in my soul by PTSD.

If only one person benefits from the revelations in this book,

I would consider it to be a success. I realize some have had it worse than me, and that mine may be a different form of the disease than that which plagues many soldiers. I cannot promise that you will find all the answers and that is because sometimes we do not know all the questions. The good news is that there is hope.

In the distance I see a tree. It is a marvelous and a beautiful one and it's just a tree.

CHAPTER 1

UNFORGIVEN

I JUST WANT TO SEE TREES

Tortured branches reaching for the skies
Pleading for forgiveness
With tears and sighs

No leaf would dare grow on this dying tree
For un-forgiven was he

Prayers ignored and clemency denied
The tree was left alone and alone it died.

Just like the Soldier with a heavy heart and broken soul
That came back from war intact, but never whole

Pleading for forgiveness with a tear in his eye
He was left alone and alone he would die, because
Just like the tree un-forgiven was he.

~ By Marc Raciti

* * *

HAWAII 2007

EIGHTEEN YEARS OF DEDICATED AND selfless service to the United States Army. I had deployed five times and had seen more horrors than any man should have to bear in one lifetime. I had cared for the wounded, mourned for the dead and consoled the survivors to the point that I was numb. I had written too many death certificates and zipped-up too many body bags. The stress of it all had taken the heaviest toll on my family. I was alone in Hawaii. My wife and I were no longer getting along and she chose to stay in San Antonio with the children. I could no longer communicate with her and she didn't understand or acknowledge my pain.

One evening I found myself wanting aimlessly along Hawaii's North Shore silently wondering "Will this be the night I end it all?" I whispered to myself. In the end, I was afraid—not of dying, but of living.

"I'm such a coward," I mumbled to myself while staring at the tree.

The Hawaiian North Shore winds blew a cool breeze that evening, with sporadic breaks between gusts of air. The treetop was the only thing visible from the highway. The rest of the tree was hidden below the arch of the bridge. Selecting this tree was easy since it offered concealment, was easy to access, and was close to home. People driving on this road probably never even saw the tree. Perhaps they would catch a glimpse of its top branches, then quickly dismiss it as not worthy of further attention.

The tree's outer branches held sparse smaller ones that were bare and gray, like fingers reaching upward toward the sky, while the lower branches were thick arms that extended out from the wide trunk as if offering me a welcoming hug. The stripped down tree, weathered by wind, rain and the passage of time, indicated a certain type of vulnerability. However, up close, I recognized the strength in its colossal central trunk.

It seemed to me the tree and I had a lot in common—we'd both been through a lot, and we were ready to give up. We were forgotten, alone, and sad. The tree stood alone under the bridge and I stood alone in the world.

I called this tree "Unforgiven" because it seemed strange to me that this tree and no other in its vicinity appeared diseased or dying. Birds would not even perch on its branches. It was as if God himself had punished this tree with a long and lifeless existence. I understood what it was like to exist without life or hope and, yet, be unable to die. I knew that how I was feeling inside was probably a lot like how this tree looked. My soul was bare and my heart heavy. I felt empty and worthless.

Similar to "Unforgiven", people would pass me by with barely a glimpse, looking right through me, as if I were not there. For my part, I rarely initiated eye contact, hoping to avoid the awkward or uncomfortable expressions on the faces of those who feared being dragged into my misery. If I did happen to catch someone's gaze, it wasn't hostility I encountered— that would imply an emotion—it was indifference. Sometimes it is easier not to know the truth and move on.

Part of this isolation was my own doing. I had pushed my friends and family as far away from me as possible. My mind swirled with a constant barrage of thoughts convincing me that I was undeserving of love and care. And, now, at the foot of "Unforgiven", those relentless thoughts told me that the strap in my hand was the ultimate solution—the strap that was tied into a noose.

I had planned this for several weeks. Like most people who consider suicide, I did not want to give anyone any indication of my plan in advance. I wanted people to say, *"Wow I did not see that one coming."*

My mind was made up, and all necessary arrangements were made, such as my last will and testament and a medical directive with a "do not resuscitate" order. I wrote letters to my three children attempting to explain my reasons for ending my life, figuring my two adult daughters would probably understand much better than my teenaged son. These notes were the hardest of things to write, but it was my hope that providing them with answers might offer them closure in the end.

The sun had set and the wind was blowing more consistently now. Dark clouds were moving in rapidly and there was very little warning before raindrops pelted the ground around me. Standing there in the rain staring at old "Unforgiven", I found myself unable to take a step forward and lacking the courage to do what I had set out to do.

This left me feeling even more worthless and helpless. Now cowardice was added to the list. My jeep was parked just a short walk up the highway at the Dole Cannery not far from the bridge. The decision was made. Not tonight.

I placed the strap in my cargo pocket and made it up the hill, the soaking rain making my decision that much easier. On the drive back, my mind raced with flashes of faces—some of family and friends, others of the dead. My heart was full of anger and disappointment in myself for being unable to carry out a simple task.

This amount of frustration and self-loathing only fueled my resolve. I went home and started to plan for another day to end my life.

Several weeks passed, and I still could not muster the courage to make good on my plan. Some days I would stop on my way home from work and go down to "Unforgiven" and just sit there for hours with my back against the trunk, nestled down in the tree's roots as if I was sitting in a big armchair. Somehow the tree seemed to understand my pain and this thought gave me comfort.

While resting in the tree's nurturing embrace, I allowed my thoughts to turn to my three children and wife, thinking how much happier we were when I was whole, before the fights, the tears, the anger, and the resentment. That time when life was much simpler, when we were so poor I worked part-time nights and weekends to make ends meet, waiting tables at the local Howard Johnson's. Sometimes I would have just enough tip money leftover that I could afford to take the girls to Baskin Robbins for ice cream. We didn't have cable television, we survived on beans and rice for weeks at a time. We'd even sneak popcorn and drinks into the dollar movie theater. Somehow, I remember these as being happier times. Despite the hardships, we were together and we were happy.

As I lay there reminiscing about the past, my thoughts suddenly turned on me. I became angry and resentful. They told me I did not deserve a family or any happiness, only the sadness and isolation that would end in early death. How would my suicide impact their lives? I asked myself. Will I be missed by anyone? Did I explain in enough detail my feelings of hopelessness and sadness? Would they understand and, more importantly, would they forgive me?

Tears streamed down my cheeks. I was unable to move. Then my thoughts turned again, this time to "Unforgiven". I wanted to understand what happened to it. This once magnificent tree was probably covered with healthy green leaves that danced in the wind in its original days of glory, brimming with branches full of life and flowers that bloomed year-round. At one time, it provided great shade and shelter for smaller animals.

What had happened to it? There were other trees in the area that were thriving. How come they were spared, but not this one? Or was the tree like me? Was it somehow punishing itself?

As my eyes grew heavier, I leaned back and looked up into the star-filled sky. The beautiful crisp air filled with sea surf and the sweet aromatic scent of the nearby plumeria trees had a calming effect on me. The sound of the waves crashing on the North Shore was rhythmic and soothing. My mind began to slowly settle down. The thought of getting up and going back to my place crossed my mind, but there was nothing waiting for me at home.

Sitting on the moist ground at the base of "Unforgiven" made me feel good. If I were sitting on a comfortable chair, the guilt would have been too much and I probably would have gotten up. But, sitting in the dirt made it okay to feel good, even if it was only for a moment.

Now I could feel myself drifting away and the sound of the waves becoming fainter as I sank into sleep. The dreams I had as I slept there were vivid but surreal. In one, I was walking toward "Unforgiven", and as I got closer to the tree I saw myself sitting still, lifeless, in the exact spot where I'd fallen asleep. I had no expression on my face, but my eyes appeared sad and in a downward gaze. The longer I stood there looking at myself, the less I would see of me. I was slowly becoming part of the tree—another root outside the ground.

The drizzle of a light rain woke me up or perhaps it was the dream. Did I die in my sleep at the base of "Unforgiven" and then become part of it? I shook my head to take away the sleep and gain my bearings. Then my thoughts turned to how far I had fallen, convinced that I deserved to sink to this low level. Just for a moment, I caught a glimpse of the old me in my mind: a great husband, father, soldier and American—the version of myself I no longer recognized. Now, all that was left was a man plagued by survivors' guilt, unidentified anger, and profound sadness.

I was a man who had worked my way up through the Army ranks from private to field grade officer and medical provider. I had raised myself up by my bootstraps, tirelessly pushing myself to improve. I had been determined to make it through college—mostly by attending night school after working all day as a soldier—while holding down a part-time job. I made a decent living and I secured a future for my children. But, in spite of all of this, I had lost my family, mostly by my own doing.

The self-destruction of my life was slow and methodical, and all because I did not believe I deserved things such as a loving family, a comfortable life, or a successful career. Fallen soldiers and friends who did not come home from Iraq would never have those things, so how was it okay for me to enjoy my life, knowing they would never see their loved ones or home again? I felt like a fraud.

I rose to my feet and headed to my Jeep feeling sore but somewhat rested. In an instant, a feeling came over me. It was the courage to make one more attempt at suicide. I pulled the strap from the cargo pocket of my uniform, and headed back toward the tree. I tied the strap around one of the main branches and then slipped the noose around my neck.

The words "FUCK THEM ALL!" slammed through my brain. Sucking in one last breath of life, I walked right off the main branch that was about 10 feet off the ground and waited for the noose to tighten and my neck to snap. Strangely, everything seemed to happen in slow motion. I fell so slowly that I had time to look up through the branches above me and beyond to the night sky. The noose finally started to tighten around my neck.

In a few more seconds it would all be over, I told myself. No more guilt, sadness, despair or self-loathing. I kept waiting for whatever was supposed to be greeting me on the other side to appear—an angel, a white light, any of the things I'd read about that appear when people die. Instead, my body hit the ground like a sack of potatoes. My spine felt like it had migrated through my chest. The impact of hitting the ground jolted me awake.

At that moment I realized I had only been dreaming. I felt sad that I was still alive, but, at the same time, happy I wasn't dead. The emotion was hard to define. It was like losing a shitty parent. On the one hand, you are sad they are gone, but on the other hand, you're happy they can't make anyone miserable anymore.

The following day I had early clinic on Schofield Barracks, so making it to Starbucks early enough to get coffee was important, considering the long day of patient care ahead of me.

Nothing seemed unusual for a Monday, but I could tell that something was not right. It was as if everybody knew what had happened to me the night before. Paranoia crept in with every glance and with any conversation that didn't directly involve me. All I could think about was that my colleagues had found out my dirty secret and now I was going to have to explain why I'd tried to kill myself.

As the day went on, I grew more and more anxious until by the end of my shift I was shaking with fear and could not wait to get out of there. But, oddly enough, nobody came to talk to me about anything other than clinic stuff. Every time someone showed up at my door, I thought it might be my commander or someone with authority coming to apprehend me. For what, I did not know.

Finally it was 4 p.m. and time for everyone to go home which gave me the opportunity to relax a bit and go over my emails for the day. In my inbox there was a message from my branch manager with the subject line "Let's talk about your next deployment." A chill went down my spine as I read that. I had just returned from a deployment and now they were talking about sending me again?

The message was very short but to the point: "*Marc, I know you just got back, but I need someone with your skillset to go again. David had a heart attack and is not able to return for this deployment. Can you fill in for him until he recovers? I will owe you big time. Let me know if you are willing to go again and I will take care of everything else.*"

After reading that email, my feelings of anxiety and paranoia were suddenly gone. All I felt now was relief and excitement, ultimately culminating in euphoria The pressure of committing suicide was lifted off my shoulders. I was being deployed to a really bad place and that meant there was a high likelihood that I'd be killed by someone—or something—else.

In more recent years I have learned that it's referred to as "passive suicide" when you force the hand of fate in this way. This method of ending your life is very popular with soldiers who lose the nerve to commit suicide. We've all read about or heard stories of people being chased by police and then pulling out a plastic gun when cornered, pressuring the police to open fire, thus, placing the burden of death in someone else's hands.

In my case, I believed returning to the battlefield would allow me the opportunity to die with dignity while supporting the war on terror and protecting our country's freedom. I would die a soldier's death which was more appealing than hanging myself.

CHAPTER 2

NOTHING WRONG WITH ME

JULY 2007 SEVERAL WEEKS BEFORE DEPLOYING

I WAS IN TROUBLE AND really needed to talk to someone—anyone—about what was going on with me. My suicide attempt had failed, and now I was waiting to deploy so the enemy could take care of what I could not. On a conscious level, my thoughts prompted me to seek professional help because I didn't really want to hurt myself. However, on the subconscious level, my mind insisted these thoughts were just bullshit and I really DID want to end my life.

Finding someone trustworthy to talk to was a difficult process because nobody seemed to fit the bill. I spent several hours researching providers, but the options were limited at Schofield Barracks. Ultimately, it looked like I had four choices, and I was able to narrow it down to one who seemed to have good qualifications, but I was concerned that he was not a veteran and had never been in combat.

I was apprehensive about discussing personal and painful memories with someone who hadn't been in combat because they might not understand what I was experiencing. It would make it that much tougher to talk things through. I was also a little self-conscious about going to the Soldiers Assistance Center (SAC) for help because there would be many junior soldiers there.

As a higher ranking officer, I felt that I might be taking a valuable spot that could have gone to a soldier more in need. The mantra of the three M's of leadership played loudly in my head: "My Mission, My Soldiers, Myself." It is difficult to be a leader and have to sit in a waiting room among your subordinates. Somehow I felt I would be judged or viewed as a weak leader.

Another reason I was hesitant about making the appointment was because I worked in the same clinic, and I worried that someone from work would see me going to the SAC for help and lose confidence in my skills as a clinician. More than anything, though, I feared the doctor would find something seriously wrong with me, like a tumor, or tap into what was bothering me and determine I was way too screwed up to continue my military service.

In the end, all these fears and apprehensions were nothing but excuses, so I finally made an appointment for 3:30 p.m. I knew the clinic turned into a ghost town by 4 p.m. and by arriving toward the end of the day I would avoid running into staff, superiors or anyone else who might judge me.

As an extra safety precaution, I decided I would show up in civilian clothes in hopes of further increasing my chances at remaining anonymous.

On the day of my appointment, my shift moved more slowly than usual. I kept looking at my watch because it would be bad form to be late for my first appointment. I was also having mixed emotions—hoping that someone would finally be able to help me, but still convinced that suicide might be my best solution. I tried to find justification to cancel but now that I'd made the appointment, there was no turning back.

Same-day cancellation is heavily frowned upon in the military. Cancellations have to be made a full day in advance, or the timeslot goes to waste because appointments are not filled at the last minute. A report stating that you cancelled your appointment is then generated and sent to your commander and you have to explain why you failed to attend your appointment.

This goes not only for mental health but for any medical appointment. If you land on this list several times and are unable to provide a good reason, you can be punished. This was not the kind of attention I wanted to draw to myself. Cancellation was not an option.

Toward the end of my shift that day, I started imagining how the consultation would go, the types of questions the doctor might ask, and how much I should reveal. Too much information could place me on suicide watch while too little could leave the impression that my condition wasn't that serious after all. I also pondered whether I was ready to share my experiences with someone who may not know what I was talking about.

For the most part, people who suffer from PTSD do not like to share what they've been through with people who never deployed. The assumption is that they do not know or understand what we have been through; and, therefore, are not worthy of knowing our sorrow.

Three o'clock came at last and I was off to see my doctor. I arrived in the waiting room of the clinic 15 minutes early and was told by the desk clerk to sit down until my name was called. Sitting among other soldiers made me realize the magnitude of this problem. The room was packed with service members from all walks of life who were silently watching CNN or playing games on their cell phones.

It was obvious that many of them had been in trouble with their unit and had a command referral, because their rank had been removed and they were accompanied by an escort. They would likely be discharged from the military either for disciplinary or administrative reasons within a few weeks.

I could hear several conversations going on at once but could not focus on a single one. There was some sporting event on the television where an announcer with a high-pitched voice was blathering on about something important only to him. I realized that wearing civilian clothing didn't really matter in the end. We lived in a small Army community in Hawaii and people would recognize me no matter what I was wearing.

Just as I had that thought, a soldier looked over at me with a knowing smile and nod. I thought he might be a patient of mine but I couldn't be sure. I only knew that his face seemed familiar. I immediately started playing some card game on my phone, keeping my head down to avoid further eye contact. After 20 minutes my name was finally called.

"MAJOR RA-Cite-EEE!" the front desk clerk called out loudly in her big-girl voice, butchering my last name as was often the case. Or maybe it just seemed that much louder because I was trying to be incognito.

Thanks to the military custom of addressing everyone by rank and last name, now my cover was really blown.

The doctor greeted me and walked me back to his office. About midway down the long corridor I could hear a soldier crying through one of the doors. He was sobbing between the words, "I saw him die right in front of me." There is nothing worse than to hear a soldier cry, but I knew where he was coming from. I almost did an about-face and walked out, but something kept me there.

I felt sorry for that poor guy in that room. I did not see his face nor recognize his voice—

I did not have to. It was the same cry I have heard come from me; the same I once witnessed in Iraq when a team of soldiers was praying to God and crying over the loss of their battle buddy. I had heard that cry way too often in my years as a soldier. It's the cry that comes from deep inside one's soul. The kind of cry that once you finish your head hurts, but somehow you feel just a little bit better. And a little more numb.

We arrived at the doctor's office and he offered me a seat in front of his desk. I sat there in silence for a minute, maybe more, watching him type away at his computer and wondered when our session would begin. After a bit longer, he looked at me over the top of his computer and asked for my name. I started to answer, but he turned his focus back to the computer almost immediately and continued typing away.

I did not say a word. Instead, I sat there staring at him, studying the wrinkles on his forehead, his receding hairline and the way his glasses sat tightly on the tip of his nose forcing multicolored nose hairs to stick out. On the rare occasion he made eye contact, he raised his nose up to peer at me through his bifocals. I am sure he could tell from the look on my face that I was getting pissed off.

After several more minutes, he stopped typing and said: "How long have you been depressed?"

I looked at him and said with a lot of reservation: "A long time, doc."

This time, he didn't bother to raise his eyes in my direction. I came to the conclusion that this guy was a jerk-off. Sitting there listening to the never-ending keyboard strokes, my heart started to sink into my chest as a feeling of hopelessness came over me. The doctor's bedside manner was poor and his attitude indifferent.

My appointment was set for an hour but I was sure we'd only spent about half an hour together—him typing away and me sitting there getting more and more pissed off. I sat there trying to calm down but found myself stewing in anger. After several more tension-filled moments had passed, he asked if I had an anger problem. I don't remember responding. I think I just stared at his stupid face and thought about the fact that if he sneezed his nose hairs would blow out of there like a noisemaker on New Year's Eve. The thought made me smile to myself.

My amusement was short-lived. The clock on the doctor's office wall was five minutes slow and I could not wait to get out of his office. The consultation could not have gone worse. All of the fears that had originally prevented me from seeking help were confirmed in a single one-hour session with a doctor who couldn't care less if I was depressed or suffering from PTSD.

Finally, the time was up. He stood and offered to walk me to the front desk, all the while making silly small talk about how excited he was to get home that evening because his wife was cooking baked ziti. He then punctuated this thought by licking and smacking his lips as if to visually demonstrate how good her food tasted. As he did so, I smiled politely as I thought to myself, what kind of grown man would make that stupid fucking face?

Once in the lobby, he set up another consultation for two weeks away before I even realized what had happened.

I went downstairs to my office and sat there for a while reflecting on what had just taken place. I could not believe the awful service I had just received from this provider. One word came to mind: malpractice. I also started thinking about the 19-year-old soldier with severe PTSD who has the great misfortune of being sent to a doctor like the one I'd just seen. No wonder we off ourselves. No wonder we feel hopeless and helpless. No wonder the United States military has the highest suicide rate per capita of any subcategory in our nation.

I couldn't help but keep replaying the soldier's cries in my head that I'd overheard at the clinic. I found myself wondering how this doctor would have handled something like that. I also wondered if that soldier would even think about opening up to a guy like him. My next thought was that I still had to endure another appointment with him. I hoped he'd just had a bad day. I have never understood why medical professionals would treat their patients this way.

As a clinician myself, I always taught my Physician Assistant students that there are only two things allowed in medicine: humility and compassion. I always stressed the importance of having a good bedside manner.

The following consultation started the same way with the doctor asking me the same questions. The awkward silence loomed in the room for several minutes, but it seemed like hours. Finally, I had to say something. I was tired of counting the lines in his head.

"Doc, do you think you can pull yourself away from that computer for a moment to hear what I have to say?" I said. "I mean, the last time you typed the whole time and you did not ask me anything, so can we talk? Or is this the way it is supposed to go?"

I could see his shoulder tensing up as he slowly turned around. I hadn't intended for my question to be inflammatory, but I wasn't upset that it was taken that way. A part of me wished for an unpleasant response so I would have an excuse to tell him to fuck off. He stopped typing and looked at me in disbelief.

"How about you be the patient and be patient?" he said. "I have to type all this stuff about you into the computer. I promise I will get to you."

He smiled with his mouth but not with his eyes. I could tell I was annoying him and that gave me some satisfaction, although I understood that getting under his skin was not the best way to get his attention. I decided I would start talking and maybe something I said would catch his ear, and he would finally start asking me questions. Basically I ended up talking to myself since he still didn't raise his head up from his computer.

At the half-hour point, our session nearly ended with me walking out abruptly, but at the last minute I decided to wait a bit longer in hopes that something— anything—would happen. I could not believe this was the system we had in place for soldiers. Our government and the military spent millions of dollars on initiatives to help soldiers overcome depression and receive treatment for PTSD and this was the best we had to offer?

As both a clinician and a soldier I was ashamed of the quality of care we were giving our soldiers. I knew there had to be someone who was a better fit for me than this guy. He did not even pretend to give a shit.

I had yet another appointment to attend two weeks later and the only thing that kept me motivated to return was the fear of getting in trouble with my superiors for canceling. I pretty much dreaded every hour leading up to it.

The third visit I walked in with a lot of attitude because, at this point, I really did not care what he had to say. I waited for him to settle down behind his computer, and, once the small talk was out of the way, I started talking about "Unforgiven" and how I really liked that tree because it reminded me of myself. I told him how I'd spent a night sleeping at the base of that tree. I told him I tried killing myself and I had failed. I told him about my plan to off myself passively during my upcoming deployment to Iraq.

As expected, the good doctor kept typing. I was appalled by his lack of care and professionalism. When he did stop typing, his only response to all that had poured out of me was one question: "Do you need a refill on your meds?"

I smiled and waited for him to start typing again. Once he did, I got up and quietly walked out of his office. If this was the best the Army had to offer then there was nothing wrong with me.

The week prior to my departure was filled with errands and tasks, none of which were fun or easy. The pre-deployment process is typically the same at every post. It is very well organized and structured. The only difference this time was that I wasn't planning on coming home alive. Since my intent was to return from Iraq in a body bag, these mundane tasks were rendered meaningless.

There was one question on a questionnaire from my unit that did stand out, however: "What do you want buried with you?" I had never seen this before so I thought it was odd and I really didn't care whether I was buried, cremated or if my remains ever made it back home at all. I only wanted a soldier's death—one that was worthy and honorable.

In the blank space provide, I wrote: "I want my Comanche scalping knife in my right hand and the blood of my enemy dried on my hands and clothes."

In retrospect, I realize I must have been out of my mind to write down some crazy shit like that. The Judge Advocate General

(JAG) Officer reviewing my paperwork was smiling, clearly amused by what I wrote. I could tell he wanted to make a comment or a smartass remark but quickly changed his mind once he looked into my already dead eyes. My expression and body language told him I was serious and disturbed. He signed my clearance papers and my last will and testament.

"Keep it somewhere safe," was all he said, offering me a tight-lipped smile and a nod.

I shook my head and walked out of the out-processing center.

One week later, I was preparing to board a plane to Iraq.

The unit I would be joining was located at Forward Operating Base (FOB) McHenry in Hawija in Northern Iraq—an area that, at the time, was reputed to be the most violent since its residents were still very loyal to Saddam Hussein.

Because of this, the unit had been very busy with incoming casualties from both sides. To prepare us for what we were about to experience, we were herded into a conference room for question-and-answer sessions with soldiers reporting on conditions in Hawija. Their stories were of austere living conditions and frequent mortar and rocket attacks on McHenry. One soldier likened Hawija to the Wild West, citing daily encounters with small arms fire and/or improvised explosive devices (IEDs).

As I listened, I looked around the room taking in the expressions of the young soldiers around me, all of whom pretended not to be affected by the horrors of war, but anyone could see they were shaking in their boots. Their faces were a reflection of my own internal guilt, anger and isolation. Even though I felt myself getting excited about—and even welcoming—the possibility of death this tour might provide, part of me was also afraid. I covered my true feelings and just smiled.

Like all deployments, this one was a game of hurry-up-and-wait filled with the uncertainty of not really knowing what day or time we would be leaving. The only clues came when lock downs and restrictions were put in place several days prior to our departure.

Part of these advance preparations involved pinpointing the most senior ranking soldier and naming him movement commander, also known as "flight babysitter." This assignment gave some poor schlep additional responsibilities during the flight, but offered no real power and losing someone along the way could seriously affect his career.

Thank God there was one guy who outranked me by a few months, and, boy, did he want that job. His eyes shifted anxiously when he asked what my date of rank was and he was super relieved when he realized that his was earlier than mine. I was equally as happy to sit back and let him organize and try to control all those troops

Once officially "in charge," he became condescending, obnoxious and loud— the kind of person who would snap his fingers to get your attention while he called you "hero" or "sport," offering back-handed compliments like "Not bad for a loser." I even saw him belittle a platoon sergeant in front of his soldiers. This guy was out of control and obviously had no respect for the non-commissioned officer corps or enlisted personnel. I really did not like the way he spoke to anyone—me included.

With the selection of movement commander out of the way, the next step was to pair everyone up so that we were accountable for our partners and less likely to get lost. I got lucky as hell when I was paired up with Lance. He was a crusty chief warrant officer (CW3) and, like most of them, he knew all the ins and outs of the Army. Additionally, he knew all the dirt on most of our people and, pretty much, the scoop on just about everything else.

The trip to Kuwait was long. Despite my normally poor sleeping habits, I somehow managed to fall asleep. I had just drifted off when the movement commander woke me up to ask if I had any meds that would help him sleep. What an asshole! I thought to myself. Here he was waking ME up to give HIM something to sleep. I quickly decided a little payback was in order. I reached into my aid bag and pulled out a pink-colored pill and told him to take it with at least a liter of water. And, just for good measure, I winked at him and said, "It's the good stuff."

He nodded as if he understood what the good stuff was, and

said, "This is not going to get me in trouble with a piss test is it?"

I gave him a reassuring smile and said, "It's just to help you sleep."

As he was walking back to his seat I reminded him to drink at least a liter of water.

Truth be told, I didn't have any controlled substances with me. My unit had already been in Iraq for some time, and they'd taken all medications with them. After my exchange with the soldier, Lance, the warrant leaned over and in a west Texas accent said, "Did you give that boy Benadryl?"

I nodded and replied, "And lots of water."

We broke out in laughter, knowing the Benadryl would definitely make that soldier sleepy, but he'd also be getting up to pee all night.

"Well, ya gotta stay hydrated," I said.

About midway through the flight, I woke up to a dark cabin with the sound of engines humming. I looked around me at the young faces of the sleeping soldiers. Some did not seem old enough to be in the Army, let alone fight in a war. Then my thoughts turned to my kids and I wondered if they would ever understand me. My laptop was full of partially written letters trying to explain why I hadn't come back alive. They were way more difficult to finish than you can imagine.

I began a new letter to my kids explaining my thoughts as plainly as possible. After that, I wrote letters to my remaining family and the friends I was still in contact with. This was a rapidly diminishing number since I'd pushed the majority of my loved ones away.

These letters had to be different than the ones I had prepared the night I tried to hang myself. Those letters were written to convey my fear of living. This time I wanted to convey a more heroic tone and explain that I'd met my fate in combat and died for my country, sacrificing myself for the freedoms of our nation.

* * *

"Dear Children,

If you are reading this it's because I did not make it back. Now, I realize this is probably very hard to accept but know that I'm in a much better place now. I do not know the details of my demise but as a soldier in a time of war I can imagine I was killed in action. I want you kids to know that I served my country honorably and without reservation. I went to war willingly in support of the Global War on Terror, and I would do it over again. Having said that, I wanted to impart one last bit of wisdom to you and I hope it serves you well. Please understand that what I'm saying is not always what I have done myself. I think a much better version of myself could pull this off better, but this is the way I should have lived my own life. Blood is thicker than water. I want you to always remember that. Family comes before any friend. So, take care of one another and yourselves. Live healthy and take care of your bodies. You want to be fit and healthy because when the chips are down, at least you have your health. Never start smoking and don't take drugs. Never lose control of yourself. That is when bad people around you will try to take advantage of you. Read the Bible and go to church, and take care of your mother. She and I had our problems, but she is a good woman and she will need you now more than ever. Find your passion in life and become your dreams, because life is too short for regret. Make good decisions. Do not let anyone push their inadequacies or their fears onto to you and your dreams. Don't conform yourself to mediocrity, otherwise that is what you will become and all three of you are far from mediocre. Don't take shortcuts in life— it will only leave you half-fulfilled and lacking in content. Choose the hard right instead of the easy left every time. You will not be disappointed in yourself in the end. Stand on your own two feet. Never be dependent on anyone else for your happiness or your own decisions in life. Don't use foul language. People will judge you for what you say and how you look—always. Don't give anyone that power over you. Remember if you are about to do something and you wonder if it is a good idea, it probably isn't. I love you kids with all my heart and I will watch over you from above. I will ask to be your guardian angel, that way I will always be with you. Your loving father."

* * *

By writing these letters, it was my intention to share pearls of wisdom with my children and codes they could live by. However, the truth is, I wrote them more for me than for them. I felt guilty for not wanting to return to them alive and this was evident in the hollow and insincere words I'd written that painted a picture of an altruistic man who'd had no control over his own demise. Deep down I knew I wouldn't be dying a hero's death. I'd be purposely putting myself in harm's way in order to accomplish what I'd been unable to do at the foot of "Unforgiven". Suicide by passive means is still suicide. Instead of writing letters explaining my fear of living, I'd written about my fear of dying.

Because I was new to the unit, I didn't know many people. This made it hard to find someone I could trust enough to deliver the letters once I'd passed. The commander and a few of the medics were great acquaintances of mine, but to expect them to take on this responsibility was a lot to ask of someone. I placed them in addressed envelopes. For now, the letters would be safe with me. If I were to get killed, someone would find them and know what to do with them. That was my plan for the moment, until I could trust someone enough to deliver them to my family.

CHAPTER 3

THE LOST

HAWIJA, IRAQ 2007

THE FIRST TIME I GOT mail from my unit back home was three months into my deployment. It is a huge thing for soldiers to get a care package or even a handwritten letter while they're away from home. Everybody gets email these days while deployed, but it's not the same thing as handwritten correspondence. I simply cannot emphasize enough how important it is for a soldier to receive a piece of mail from a loved one.

I remember avoiding the mail truck a lot of the time because I did not want to be disappointed yet again when there were no letters waiting for me, but on this day I got lucky. When I returned to my Combat Housing Unit (CHU), I found a small box from my hospital unit back home had been delivered.

For the uninitiated, CHUs are lovely short singlewide trailers that house anywhere from one to eight soldiers at a time depending on your rank. Those with higher ranks get a CHU to themselves, while lower ranking soldiers are packed in like sardines. Because I was a field grade officer I shared my CHU with only one other person—a battalion surgeon named Sam.

In the desert, you have to keep your A/C very cold in order to kill the sand flies, so your CHU feels like a meat locker. In addition, the windows are covered with sand bags and the entire exterior of the unit is piled high with 2x4 palettes meant to brace the walls and roof of the unit in the case of incoming mortar attacks. When you're inside you're entirely in the dark and rely heavily on fluorescent lighting. It makes you feel like an armadillo trapped in an insulated metal container.

Sam's wife often sent popcorn in care packages and we had a hot plate for boiling water, so as you can imagine, our frigid, airtight rabbit hole was always pretty stale to say the least. It basically smelled like a combination of popcorn, ramen noodles and ass at all times.

In the center of the room was a table dividing the CHU into sides and on it we had our computers set up to play "Command and Conquer" which was our go-to game for killing time.

On this particular day, however, I couldn't be distracted. I was too focused on opening the package from home. I took my time, savoring the moment. I opened the box with precision, making sure address labels were carefully preserved so I could send thank-you notes to those who had taken the time to reach out.

After sifting through well wishes from people in my clinic, I pulled the bubble wrap out of the box and spent about five minutes popping it. For some reason the sounds of those pops brought me extreme pleasure. Beneath the wrap, there were several magazines, including a Harley Davidson motorcycles magazine and a Maxim with some hot chick on the cover.

Under the magazines, I found a note wishing me a happy holiday accompanied by a Ziploc bag containing toothpaste and razors and a CD titled "This is what we have been up to in your absence." I was skeptical as I slipped the disc into my computer. Seconds later, a very well put together slideshow appeared on my screen showing images of all the people, both military and civilian, who worked at the clinic in Hawaii.

They were all happy, smiling, and enjoying their freedom, some even playing golf or enjoying a cookout on the beach. I hardly knew anyone in those pictures—most of them seemed to be new to the clinic. I couldn't help but think it all seemed very impersonal and insincere because everyone who was deployed got a similarly generic disc in their care package.

Although I understood the CD was sent with the best of intentions, but it only made me feel like shit. I realized that the CD was nothing more than a check-the-box kind of thing, where someone was tasked to compile photos to send to all the soldiers deployed to Iraq. The CD played for several minutes before I reached my maximum capacity for bullshit and turned it off. It was like watching a happy PR campaign. It was simply too painful to watch. It made me angry because I felt like it was insensitive to send something like that to me knowing that I could not do any of those things. I was even angrier because they too were soldiers and I couldn't understand why they weren't deployed.

The slideshow also served as a reminder that I'd come to Iraq in hopes of being killed, and I was becoming more and more frustrated, because missions were fewer and farther between, now that our tour was coming to an end. I wanted something drastic to happen before we had to return home. I wished I had never put that disc into my computer. It was a slap in the face to those of us who lived in austere conditions, eating the same crappy food day in and day out, to be forced to sit there and watch such insincere nonsense.

In response, I decided to make a CD of my own to send back to show them what I was up to during the bloodiest month in Iraq. I hoped that the images of our poor living conditions left them feeling as sick to their stomachs as their thoughtless, happy-go-lucky presentation had made me.

* * *

It wasn't long after opening that care package that I set off on my campaign of isolation. It was a calculated and methodical process. Starting with my loved ones, I stopped answering emails and writing letters, and I cut off any communication at all with folks back home. I stopped socializing with the other officers, begging off going to the weekly fellowship nights my commander set up where we'd all gather to binge on episodes of "Rescue Me" or "The Shield." My commander would sometimes make a point to find me the next day and say I'd been missed, but to no avail.

My evenings and days were spent alone inside. My CHU had become my sanctuary. Eventually, I even started taking my meals back to my CHU instead of eating in the mess hall. Sam grew increasingly concerned and made attempts to distract me with computer games or trips to the gym, but my downward spiral toward becoming a lost soul was well underway. To his credit, he never quit trying despite the fact that my hard headedness was visibly frustrating him.

During this time, I also started volunteering for riskier missions outside the wire in hopes of fulfilling my death wish. I knew it was a matter of probabilities—the more often I went out there, the higher the likelihood that I'd get hurt or killed. Up until this point, Sam and I had been splitting up these duties but I told him I would take over his shifts from now on. After all, he was recently married with a baby on the way.

Me? I just wanted to be done. My commander dealt me a blow, however, and insisted that my skills were more useful on base. I was stuck with no choice but to retreat to my CHU and hope to be struck down by a mortar attack.

* * *

BATTLE CROSS FOR THE FALLEN AT FOB McHENRY 2007

Despite my isolation campaign, the relentless, gore-filled pace of life in Iraq made the six months I spent at FOB McHenry fly by. Finally, it was time to go home. The flight home was uneventful, but it felt like the longest day of my life. I spent the entire time reflecting on what I'd been through in Hawija and on the Wolfhound Wall in the middle of FOB McHenry where the names and ranks of 18 fallen brothers were painted in gold. These names would remain in my heavy heart, for they would never return home.

Among those names, was that of our final fatality in Iraq, a young man from Wahiawa, Hawaii, who I'd really connected with. We'd met one time in the mess hall when I noticed him reaching for slices of bread with dirty gloves on and his weapon still strapped to his back. He was obviously in a hurry. I joked with him, saying it wasn't very sanitary to make a sandwich with dirty gloves on, and his response cracked me up.

He said: "If you think my gloves are dirty, you should see my hands."

He then smiled and proceeded to finish making his sandwich. After that, he would stop by every Sunday for Spam Musubi, a Hawaiian-style "sushi" consisting of a small block of rice wrapped around a slice of fried SPAM and seaweed. I started out making the dish for myself, but once word got out around base, all Hawaiians knew to stop by Doc's CHU on Sundays if they wanted some.

Then one day, the young Sergeant was on a mounted patrol when his vehicle was hit by an EID. He died instantly and was brought to our Aid Station. We handled the remains and I wrote his death certificate. I was devastated to say the least.

As these memories replayed in my mind over and over throughout the flight, I couldn't help but wonder how my already fragile state of mind would be affected once I arrived back home.

Surviving my deployment left me feeling unfulfilled and unsatisfied. Now I had to deal with me.

CHAPTER 4

AMPUTATION OF THE SOUL

LOOKING BACK IT SEEMED THAT every time I returned from a deployment, there was a piece of me missing. Something within me was just no longer there—a certain piece that you only realize is missing once you see it in those around you.

The first time I felt like something was not normal was shortly after returning from my first deployment to Saudi Arabia in Support of Operation Desert Storm in 1991. Somehow my life had changed and I couldn't quite put my finger on how it had happened.

From the outside looking in, it was hard to tell that anything was different. My career was doing well and things at home were seemingly good. I was stationed at Fort Sill, Oklahoma. I had been promoted to specialist (E-4) in the Army and was being considered for promotion to sergeant.

In the end, I was promoted to corporal in consolation for not having enough promotion points, but I wore the stripes with pride and distinction, as an NCO should and was that much closer to being promoted to sergeant.

That would happen later once I left Fort Sill to go to Germany. After a few short years there I applied to the Army Physician Assistant School.

At work I managed to keep my cool most of the time, but I did have a mean streak. The soldiers that worked for me would sometimes just shake their heads in frustration when I snapped at them. They somehow knew that challenging me would probably result in more problems. At the time I did not know where all this anger came from and, in fact, probably didn't even realize I was angry at all. But the people around me sure noticed how I was. I had become a real jerk, and I was the last person to realize it.

I remember blowing up at my oldest daughter because she stuck a plastic dinosaur in my nose while I was taking a nap. Ordinarily I would have thought that was funny as hell, laughing and dismissing it as nothing. But, instead, I took it as a full-on assault on my person and a tremendous act of disrespect. In retrospect I should have taken the high road. Instead I spanked her and she soon learned to steer clear of me. It was the beginning of me scaring my family away from me. I kept pushing them away until there was nothing or nobody left. The kids stopped playing around me, and my wife just accepted it.

At the same time I was beginning to have very vivid nightmares. They became more intense as time went by, to the point where

I was often afraid to go to sleep. On those nights, I'd stay up and watch TV, pacing back and forth. Every noise outside caught my attention. Even crickets chirping outside sounded like footsteps to me. I was constantly monitoring the house like a watchdog. On the nights when my body did give in to sleep, the nightmare was almost always the same.

It would start with the Islamic evening prayer being chanted by a religious leader in the distance. The prayer would then be quickly muffled out by the sounds of alarms going off secondary to an eminent missile (SCUD) attack. At that point, I would reach into my chemical mask carrier, but my mask was never there. I would frantically search my duffle bag, but to no avail. In the background I could hear the Patriot missile system deploying to intercept these SCUD missiles. I knew I had no time to escape.

CHAPTER 5

PIECES OF ME

AFTER RETURNING FROM DESERT STORM, I was promoted to Sergeant and sent to Germany for a three-year tour with my family. There I applied to the Army Physician Assistant School and got Selected in 2004. The years passed and my symptoms were slowly worsening. My anger and depression really started affecting my family. But, I was so focused on finishing PA school and becoming an officer. I must have compartmentalized or suppressed these feelings in order to accomplish my goals.

The other reason is that I probably was not really aware that I was depressed or angry. I only knew that there was something wrong with me and I did not know what to call it.

Ten years passed before I was deployed again. I was already a commissioned officer and I owed the army six years for PA school. I was at the mid point in my career, so I'd decided to go ahead and stay in the Army to see how all this would play out. I'd already been in the service for a decade, so I figured I might as well hang in there for another and reap the benefits of retiring after 20 years.

Despite feeling overwhelmed and suffering from nightmares on a regular basis, it wasn't until my deployment to Kosovo that it really began to dawn on me why a part of me was missing. The process of this realization was insidious and had a profound impact on me once I discovered it.

CAMP ABLE SENTRY MACEDONIA 2000

I arrived at Camp Able Sentry (CAS) in Macedonia late in the evening. Our Battalion was already in Kosovo, but due to weather and scheduling, the small contingency I was traveling with had been delayed by a couple of weeks. Despite this, the military liaison troops at the reception station were well prepared for our arrival and did a great job of showing us where we could put our equipment and bed down for the evening—unlike Desert Storm where they didn't even know where to put us when we began arriving in 1990.

At CAS, we were housed in large tents, some with heaters and others without. The cold air that nipped at us all the way from the flight line to our tents was a sign that winter was upon us. I could not wait to crawl into my sleeping bag and get warm. Thankfully, I'd been assigned to a heated tent. A potbelly stove glowing a bright orange color sat in the middle of the large open space and a soldier was stationed nearby to ensure it was fueled adequately. He sat there reading a book well into the night, while other soldiers came and went around him.

Like our group, some units were just arriving at camp while

others were on their way out. Our tent was in a constant state of flux and filled with never-ending chatter. Adding to the cacophony was the slapping of the tent flap as the chilling wind blew it open and closed, and the humming of generators running continuously, not to mention the buzzing that remained in my ears from the loud aircraft we flew in on. With all of that noise, falling asleep was nearly impossible. I finally managed to drift off around one in the morning.

Toward the early morning hours, sunlight poured into the tent every few minutes as the tent flap continued to dance in the gusty wind. As I lay there listening to the flap being whipped against the side of the tent, it occurred to me how much all of this reminded me of Desert Storm. The sound of the generators and the smells of mildew and fuel from the potbelly stove were all reminiscent of my first deployment.

Trading the toasty comfort of my sleeping bag for the cold air was not appealing, but I finally dragged myself out of bed. In processing was waiting for my team to check in. Once up and moving, I thought about going to the Mess Hall to grab a bite, but I settled for a cup of coffee from the cappuccino bar near the Post Exchange to avoid the cold outdoors for as long as possible.

In spite of the frigid temperatures, I felt great all day and was excited about being in the Balkans and starting a new adventure. It wasn't until later that afternoon when I was walking around the maze of tents and port-o-potties and the sound of helicopters were buzzing overhead that it hit me: My euphoric mood was triggered by the familiarity of my surroundings—sounds, smells and anything else that reminded me of Desert Storm.

On the drive north to Kosovo I started piecing my thoughts together to better understand why this sense of familiarity was exciting me. There was little to be happy about since I was being deployed and was leaving my family behind, yet I couldn't help but notice my spirits lifting. It wasn't logical.

Then it hit me like a ton of bricks: This feeling was nothing more than reconnecting with the part of me that was lost during my first deployment. It was as if I, the prodigal son, had come home after being away for a very long time. The feeling spooked me because I never wanted to think of a deployment as a homecoming.

Up until now, I'd chalked the changes in my life up to growing pains as the result of unresolved issues from my past, or maybe even a reaction to what I'd seen in Desert Storm. After what I'd experienced in the Gulf, it seemed to make some sense that I was taking life more seriously these days. However, it wasn't just rehashing bad memories from the war. My fuse was becoming shorter and shorter over minute things. Things I once thought were funny no longer made me laugh. Smiling was something I reserved only for photos. Where I once was able to tolerate people making mistakes or saying silly things, I no longer had the patience, even when it came to my children. Life had become humorless for me.

It would not take much for me to go from 0 to 100 on the

anger scale and I found myself wanting to fight anyone who looked at me for longer than the social acceptable three-second glance. I found I was willing to physically hurt someone for very minor transgressions, perceived or otherwise.

One might argue that perhaps I'd just matured, but I don't think your personality ever really changes to that degree. Whereas, before I would genuinely love to make someone laugh or smile for no other reward than the sweet laughter and joy my humor would bring, now I would say mean things to elicit entirely different responses. It was more about pointing out ugly truths laced with anger and malice and focusing on people's faults and awkward moments rather than their virtues and gifts. Worst of all, I would direct my anger toward people who did not deserve that kind of treatment.

The anger inside made me restless and ruled my heart. Most days I was able to function without much trouble, but all it took to set me off was someone asking questions about Desert Storm, especially when someone made assumptions about a war they knew nothing about. Then I was off and running. One time at the dinner table I snapped at my stepmother for saying something negative about our participation in the war. What she didn't realize was that any criticism about a war in which I'd lost friends was disrespectful and completely inappropriate. I'd been overseas burning shit for nine months and the last thing I wanted to hear was somebody making judgments about the campaign. I was feeling edgy, to say the least, and I lashed out.

Prior to my first deployment, I don't remember ever being this easily angered. Any anger I felt was triggered by the usual stuff—the price of gas, politics or Van Halen breaking up. There was a big difference between my pre-deployment self and the person I had become.

CAMP BONDSTEEL, KOSOVO 2000

I recall seeing the best and worst of humanity all in one day. I saw the killing field and mass graves with executed Kosovo Albanians and on the same day we met an Albanian family who adopted a Serbian child to raise him as Christian. This was the plan until he could be reunited with any remaining family in Serbia.

As a newly promoted Captain in the Army I was focusing on my mission to win hearts and minds of the Kosovo Albanians and the newly displaced Serbs in the region. Again I was in my element and felt good about the things we were doing. Our job mostly consisted of Medical Civil Action missions thereby providing medical care to people in remote areas of Kachanic, Kosovo.

I loved the people. They were truly amazing, both factions, although they hated each other, but they were very welcoming to the American doctors.

My deployment to the Balkans, brought a lot of awareness and insight to my anger and depression. It made me realize the deep-rooted connection I had to being deployed and the feelings of disconnection throughout the rest of my life.

My deployment was six months long and upon my completion of this tour, I was assigned to Fort Bragg, NC. There I would start my residency in Orthopedics, which brought forth a tremendous amount of stress and again took me away from my family a great deal. I remained focused on my career but throughout my training my issues with anger continued to resurface.

CHAPTER 6

THE NEW ME

IT WAS MY THIRD DEPLOYMENT. It had only been three years since Kosovo and yet I was out there again. Still no resolution to my anger and I was no closer to figuring out what was wrong with me. The biggest difference was that in Kosovo I was trying to figure out what was wrong with me. Now, I was starting not to care.

* * *

AL RAMADI, IRAQ 2003

We slowly traveled north on Highway One from Kuwait to Al Taqaddum (TQ). That was to be the final destination for half our company, the rest would continue on to Camp Junction City or Al-Ramadi. It was early in the day but the sun was blistering.

Highway One, also known as Main Supply Route (MSR) Tampa, was the primary road used to move personnel, supplies and equipment to various points in Iraq. Although it had several protected stops along the way for all coalition forces, it was not entirely safe. Because it was the most direct route, we used it a lot during the early years of the war. Our convoy was split up into three separate smaller groups of vehicles. We left Kuwait at different times so as not to bunch up on the highway, thus minimizing the amount of casualties if we were attacked.

The group I rode in was comprised of 12 vehicles and about 30 troops, including medics and maintenance personnel. We also had six Military Police escort vehicles. The MP vehicles were not part of our unit. They were only on loan until we got to our final destination. Then they would turn back with another convoy and escort them to their destination.

This particular Military Police unit was comprised of several units from the Arizona National Guard. I learned to love and respect these soldiers for their bravery and professionalism. They protected our convoys especially during our entry from Kuwait to Iraq. They took the point by speeding up ahead and exploring any suspicious vehicles or debris along the highway. They took big risks to protect us.

My vehicle was a two-and-a half-ton truck that had seats hard as stone, poor suspension, and no air-conditioning. Inside, the cabin was dusty, hot, and offered very little room to move or stretch your legs. There were rest stops along the way, much like you would see on highways in Europe or the U.S. Overall, it was a decent highway until we got closer to Fallujah. Then it changed to mostly single lane roads. This trip would normally take several hours by car, but it took us three days in a convoy with multiple stops along the way.

THE ARIZONA NATIONAL GUARD ASSIGNED TO PROTECT OUR CONVOYS.

By mid-afternoon on the first day the sun had been pounding down on us unrelentingly for several hours as we moved through Iraq. We ate cold meals ready to eat (MRE) and drank warm water because we had no way of keeping water cold or even cool.

An officer riding in a vehicle behind us came up with the ingenious idea of wrapping a wet t-shirt around a water bottle and hanging it outside as they drove. This allowed the wind to cool the water to room temperature. It was better than drinking hot water. I really couldn't complain about a lack of chilled water though, since prior to deploying I'd seen pictures of our brothers in arms bedding down in the mud during a sandstorm.

MAIN SUPPLY ROUTE (MSR) TAMPA

Riding in extreme heat combined with the fear of being attacked, made our trip seem that much longer. I kept the window down to keep the warm air flowing. As I looked out the window toward the distance, I saw two little kids, maybe five or six years old, standing   dangerously close to the road with their arms extended motioning for food or water. I kept wondering where their parents were, while their children stood by the roadside begging for any scraps of food or water we could give them.

There had been a time when soldiers would throw MREs out of windows as convoys drove by, but the kids would run into traffic, putting themselves in harm's way to get to the food so we had to stop. Just another example of how horrible conditions had become in Iraq.

We were told to look like a hard target to show the Iraqi insurgents that we were prepared for any threat. Our orders were that we remain in full gear at all times and keep all windows rolled down with our weapons sticking out of them, but after two days of uneventful, painfully slow travel in brutal temperatures, we had become complacent and started to remove our Kevlar, flack vests, or both. We parked for the night at a rest stop called Navistar along MSR Tampa.

The stop could accommodate all our convoys in a secure compound and finally allow us to get some warm food and cool drinks. The plan was for us to stay there until early morning before pushing off to our final destination. It was difficult to get sleep, because it was still hot despite the fact that the sun had set hours ago, and no showers were available for washing away the day's dust and grime.

There were also lights on everywhere, so if you preferred to sleep in the dark, the only options were to sleep inside the cabin of the truck or under it. I found a spot on top of the truck and saw something I hadn't seen in a long time – an amazing star-filled sky. We were operating in the most austere of conditions and in the craziest situation, but in that moment I realized there was still beauty in the world.

The following morning I woke up with a splitting headache from inhaling vehicle fumes all night and from being dehydrated. It was going to be another long day. I was fortunate though, on that second day to be traveling with a sarcastically funny soldier, Sergeant Splintfield, or Splint for short. His sense of humor kept me from thinking too much about the possibility of dying, making the trip infinitely easier.

Sgt. Splint was older than the average sergeant. He had been to college and decided to join the service right after 9-11. His demeanor was different than some of the other noncommissioned officers (NCOs) I have met. He was much less uptight and a lot more confident. Along the way he told me his goal was to become a physician's assistant in the Army. A lot of medics say that, but rarely do they follow through with it. It sounds sexy to say you're going to PA School, but the program rapidly loses its appeal once you realize how hard it is to get into, much less graduate from.

I had my own personal experience to give him as an example. Splint, in spite of what I said, was sincerely interested, and since I had nothing better to do than to talk to him, we discussed in depth the last great enlisted-to-officer program the Army offered. The day passed uneventfully and we eventually stopped again for the night.

By day three we were all tired and sore from traveling. The bottom piece of my flak vest was rubbing my lower back so I removed it once again. As we rode along, we noticed our lead convoy pulled over on the side of the road. As we pulled up next to them, one of the medics waved us down and asked if I could look at one of their drivers who was complaining of back pain.

CONVOYS READY FOR DEPARTURE FROM KUWAIT TO IRAQ.

At this point we were only about 20 miles from our destination and because my specialty was in orthopedics, I was sure I would be able to help, I climbed out of the cabin of the truck to examine the soldier. Even though some of us had been deployed several times before, nothing could have prepared us for what would happen next. The reality of this war had not quite set in for me yet. But it was about to.

While I was examining the soldier I heard something that sounded like popcorn popping in the distance. I stood up and looked around the vehicle. I could not believe what I saw. About 300 meters away, men with black hoods were firing at us. I remember thinking how incredibly surreal this was. I stood there for what seemed like a couple of minutes just staring at the muzzle flashes.

"This can't be real," I mumbled under my breath. It was so surreal I felt like I was outside of my body looking down at myself, watching everything from afar as it happened, but at the same time I was moving faster than I've ever moved before. Bullets were going right through the tarp of our trucks, and people were jumping on vehicles as quickly as possible to escape.

Before I could fully process what I was seeing, the military police opened fire with their fifty-caliber weapons and grenade launchers, creating a protective shield of suppressive fire, which allowed us to move out of the kill zone. Soldiers from our convoy mounted their vehicles and started moving out quickly, however, in my mind it seemed like everything was moving in slow motion.

My brain was putting the pieces together. The machine gunner continued spraying bullets across the field in a rhythmic manner. The soldier I had been attending to got up and jumped in the back of our First Sergeant's vehicle as it was pulling away. Turning in the direction of my vehicle, I felt a warm wind blowing around me followed by airborne fragments and then a loud thud shook the ground. I was disoriented but still able to locate my vehicle. Over the sound of deafening gunfire and amidst the confusion of soldiers running everywhere I heard Sgt. Splint yell, "Sir, we need to get the fuck out of here!"

Our vehicle, which had been shielding me from the blasts, had moved leaving me completely exposed to the enemy's field of fire as I ran to where it was now parked. Sgt. Split returned fire giving me the opportunity to get to the vehicle safely. As soon as I jumped on the vehicle, he handed me his M-16 and I continued firing while he drove us out of there. As we pulled out, I kept looking out of the window to ensure we were not being fired at any more

The military police escort caught up with us several miles down the road as our convoy moved quickly to our final destination, Al Taqaddum. The road had changed from a highway to a single dirt lane leading to the back entrance of the base. Along the way to the base we saw debris— mostly boxes—strewn all over the place. From the looks of things it appeared as though another convoy had also been hit, and, in their haste to leave, they'd left food supplies scattered along the road.

At this stage, we didn't know how many soldiers had been injured in the attacks. All we knew was that one of our vehicles had been hit by a mortar and that there were no personnel in the vehicle at the time of impact.

Our battalion commander greeted us at the gate of Al Taqaddum as we pulled in. There was no time for small talk—we had wounded that needed immediate attention. Our medics started forming a triage lane as I jumped out of the truck, threw some gloves on, and got to work.

Before all was said and done, we treated 12 injured soldiers, most of whom had blast wounds from debris or had suffered injuries when scrambling to find cover. Overall, there were a few lacerations that needed suturing but otherwise we got lucky. In addition to these injuries, our company commander had developed a kidney stone due to dehydration, however he only wanted to be examined after his soldiers had been treated. He was a firm believer of the three "M's" mantra commonly used by leaders in the Army: "My mission, My men, Myself." So once I'd finished suturing my fellow soldiers, I walked him to the aid station.

As we walked, I began to feel tremendous pain in my right testicle and a sharper one at the tip of my penis. It was as if someone was slowly pushing a needle into it. My first thought was that perhaps I'd actually been stuck by a needle from a syringe set while I feverishly attended to the wounded but I didn't see or feel anything in my crotch. There was no blood. Then my lower back started to hurt.

It finally occurred to me that I also had a kidney stone and walking fast was only exacerbating the pain. I took a moment to pause alongside my Commander and, as I did so, he looked at me and said, "Are you OK, Doc?"

I started to formulate a smart aleck response but, just then, a wave of nausea rolled through my body. I barely had time to raise my index finger to indicate I needed a moment before my mouth began to water and I started vomiting (although it was more like dry-heaving since my stomach was empty). A couple of minutes passed and I started to feel less nauseous, so I was able to continue walking the remaining mile to the aid station.

HOME OF THE 101ST FORWARD SUPPORT BATTALION (FSB) CLINIC

The aid station itself was a single-story building bearing a sign with both a red crescent and a red cross indicating a treatment facility of sorts. The building looked like it may have been an infirmary at one point. The medical unit in place was comprised of several medics, a lab technician, a physician assistant, and a doctor. We were attended immediately upon arrival by the US Air Force medical staff. There was nobody else in the clinic so there was no waiting and all the attention was on us. As I lay on the table, the irony of the situation struck me. I had started out trying to take care of my commander and ended up next to him in the aid station.

The medics started fluids on us and gave us painkillers. The doctor told us to hang out there until the following day when he would further evaluate us before releasing us to our unit. During the night, they put about six liters of normal saline in me. To this day, I have never heard of anyone else receiving that much fluid with no urge to urinate, and yet I didn't wake up once to use the bathroom. That is how dehydrated I'd become.

When I woke up, my eyes were swollen and my testicles felt like they were twice their normal size because of all of the fluids my body had absorbed. I sat up on the stretcher, and tried to make conversation with my company commander.

"How are you feeling, Doc?" He asked as he was getting dressed.

I felt weak, tired and a little disoriented. The commander, on the other hand, appeared to be doing much better than the night before.

"Like shit?" He asked, in response to his own question.

I nodded.

"Well, I'm off to the unit. I'm sure they missed me." He said.

Two days later I managed to get back to my unit. I was still weak and in a lot of pain. What I would come to find out once I was sent to Baghdad for a CT scan was that I was passing a 12 mm crescent-shape kidney stone. When they saw how big it was, I was sent to Landstuhl, Germany, to have it surgically removed.

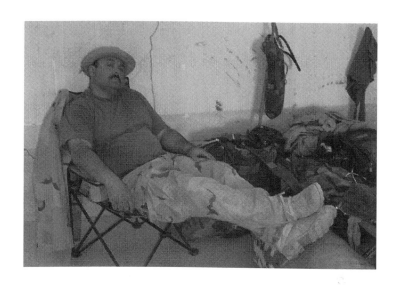

ME PASSING KIDNEY STONE

CHAPTER 7

A BRIEF REPRIEVE

TRIAGE SECTION OF THE 101ST FSB CLINIC.

AL-RAMADI, IRAQ

IT HAD NOW BEEN SEVERAL months since I'd left home, and life in Iraq was full of challenges. It was early in the days of the war, and the Army had not established all our bases or supply routes. Companies like KBR or Brown & Root had not yet been contracted to provide us with shower points, housing, laundry and dining facilities. Instead, we lived in bombed-out buildings with walls covered in blood and infested with sand flies. With every week that passed, though, new things began appearing to make our lives a little more comfortable.

By December, we moved into a refinished building which had a very functional level two-treatment facility. KBR arrived and built a dining facility that served hot food and cold drinks and our camp eventually got a small post exchange (PX) which sold snacks, soft drinks, magazines, personal hygiene items, CDs, and a modest collection of DVDs.

Even the shower situation improved.

One morning I decided to walk to a shower point about a mile away with Angry Joel who had earned this nickname because nobody could talk to him until after he'd had his morning coffee. Despite his nickname, I liked Angry Joel a lot. He was the sort of guy who didn't take any shit from anyone. The rumor on base was that there was a shower point with hot water nearby, so we wanted to investigate this miracle for ourselves.

As we made our way down the path, cool air began blowing. We realized that winter was upon us in northern Iraq, but there was no end in sight to the rain and dust storms that formed a very sticky, thick, concrete-like mud that would track everywhere. The mud was so gooey that, when you stepped into it, your foot would almost come right out of your boot.

The shower point was a half-trailer single-wide with a heater and a huge water tank. Inside, there were six to eight shower stalls with curtains and five sinks for shaving and other personal hygiene needs. Separating the showers from the sinks, was a long wooden bench for sitting or for storing your clean clothes and personal hygiene items. Only one shower was occupied when we got there.

I walked in first and the sight of dirty water and mud all over the floor crushed my hopes of the pristine shower conditions I'd been dreaming of. About an inch of water flowed in between the baseboards. I supposed we got there too late, or the word got out, and everyone had abused the site prior to our arrival.

The curtain of the occupied shower stall opened, and the soldier who'd been showering began to dry himself off.

Angry Joel was about to blow a gasket when he saw the state of that shower point.

I said to the guy, "Is there any hot water left?"

He replied with something smart like, "There is now, but not for long."

The fact that it had water was good enough for us. We sat on the edge of the opposite side of the bench and started getting ready to shower. Our side appeared to be less wet and muddy than the side on which the smart-assed guy stood. We watched him put one foot on top of the bench and then the other. Standing, he attempted to put his way-too-small sweatpants on. He tried shimmying the pants up his wet skin, but it wasn't working so he started jumping up and down to see if that would do the trick. All the while, his weiner flailed about in a circular manner much like the blades on a helicopter. Then somehow, he started drifting towards us.

Angry Joel yelled, "Ahhhhh! He's helicoptering me!"

I started to laugh and said, "Oh shit! He's helicoptering you!"

We both began laughing and simultaneously got up from our side of the bench not realizing that we were the counterbalance. As we got up, our end of the bench lifted and the shower guy landed weiner-first in that nasty pool of muddy water with his hands still glued to his hips. I have no idea why he didn't use his hands to break his fall. Sufficed to say, we heard a lot of yelling and cursing from the dirty-dick-helicopter-man but we could not stop laughing.

At that moment, the laughter felt good. It was one of those rare moments of levity that can lift your spirits in the most dire of situations, even if only temporarily.

CHAPTER 8

WE CAME HOME

AS FAR AS I COULD remember there was always something or someone who made me feel guilty. Of course being an Italian Roman Catholic did not help matters. That kind of background certainly doesn't take away from survivors' guilt, that's for sure. I remember my grandmother saying things like, "No, that's ok, I'll just stay here and drink a glass of water" when she wasn't invited to go somewhere. That sort of passive-aggressive behavior was in my blood.

But so was the need to help others. Taking care of soldiers both medically and as a leader was always my priority. Whether the soldiers were foreign or domestic, I performed my medical duties with the utmost professionalism and compassion. On many occasions I have been asked why I was treating the enemy in the same medical manner I treated our own soldiers. My response was always the same: "I took an oath to first do no harm, and all casualties are deserving of my very best."

The guilt one develops secondary to PSTD is the worst type of guilt, since you really don't understand why you feel so sad all the time—unlike my reaction to my grandmother when I understood very clearly what I felt guilty about. Survivor's guilt is not that black and white. The more you try to right a wrong, the less redemption you feel you're worthy of. The question you will never get an answer to is, "Why didn't I die instead of them?"

That thought has plagued me for years and I'm no closer to finding out the answer. The more I talk about my feelings and let my guard down, the closer I get to a certain form of closure, but never to achieving any sort of resolution to my quandary. Instead of letting go completely, I choose to hold on to the memories. It's the only thing that ties me to my fallen friends, but it also suspends me in a state of permanent guilt. It's holding on that does not allow us to move on or find answers and ultimately get better.

I remember being at a bar once and watching some off-duty soldiers walk in. They were laughing and just being themselves. My thoughts immediately turned to my fallen friends who could have been among them but weren't. But I was. Memories kept the fallen alive in my heart and the guilt was destroying my sad life.

* * *

2007, Hawaii

The flight home from Iraq to Hawaii via Germany was uneventful, but it seemed like the longest day of my life. All I could do was sit there and think about all the things I had been through on this most recent deployment. More importantly, I couldn't help but wonder how all this was going to affect my already fragile state of mind. Surviving yet another tour left me feeling unfulfilled and disappointed. I had been certain I would not be coming home alive, but now I was back to square one. I had to deal with me.

I found some comfort in saying things happened for a reason, but with no Plan B for offing myself, I felt even more lost and isolated than before. I was disappointed and relieved at the same time. The emotions I was feeling about my homecoming this time around were hard to describe. It was like being excited about receiving mail, only to find a "Dear John" letter waiting in your mailbox. I knew nobody would be waiting for me when I arrived so I just wanted to get there and bypass the whole welcoming ceremony and all that went with it.

The thought of seeing other families reunite and not my own made me incredibly sad. I had finally succeeded in pushing everyone away from me, and now when I needed my loved ones the most, they would not be there. At the same time, had they been waiting when I landed, I would have been upset that they'd come. It was a no-win situation and I had nobody to blame but myself.

* * *

We landed at Hickam Air Force Base in Hawaii early in the morning. The sun promised another temperate 78-degree Hawaiian morning. The air was filled with the scent of plumeria and pikake flowers in bloom, and the gentle ocean breeze was appealing and welcoming. I had forgotten how incredibly beautiful home could be. Somehow, despite being depressed and anxious about being back in the States, I managed to notice these subtle things that I used to take for granted.

It is amazing how little attention I'd paid to these details before I was deployed, but, then again, I am sure my altered state of mind didn't allow me to focus on such things.

After we deplaned, we were loaded onto a blue bus that took us to a welcome center. During the ride over, I fell asleep and only awakened when I heard the sound of the hydraulic brakes as the bus came to a stop. Soldiers began shuffling around and lining up to get off the bus while others peered out of the windows to catch a glimpse of their loved ones. I stayed in my seat and enjoyed the scented breeze. I was in no rush to get off the bus, since no one was waiting for me.

Before long we were ushered off the bus and into a big gym near Schofield Barracks where family members were sitting on bleachers in anticipation of our arrival. A blue-colored tarp was laid out in front of us to protect the gym floor from getting scuffed by our boots, as we filed through the doorway.

Once inside, the waiting crowd broke into pandemonium, yelling and screaming, overcome with the joy of this long-awaited moment. Children jumped up and down, too excited to sit still. Yellow ribbon posters bobbed up and down bearing welcome messages for personal heroes—a father, husband, wife, or mother —and the air smelled of detergent and coffee coming from the direction of the Family Readiness Group (FRG) table where volunteers stood guarding baked goods and refreshments.

As I stood there taking everything in, my first instinct was to call my own kids and wife, but I decided against it. Going to San Antonio to visit them would have to wait, because my mental state was not right. I couldn't help but think that maybe I didn't deserve to see them anyway.

The battalion came to attention bringing me out of my reverie. Orders were read, the chaplain offered a welcome prayer, and the division commander remarked on the bravery and gallantry we'd displayed during combat. It was not until we stood there opposite the waiting families for a good 30 minutes that we were released. As soon as that happened, relatives came running across the gym floor with tears in their eyes and profound relief as they embraced their soldier.

Shortly after everyone was reunited, an announcement boomed through a bullhorn directing all incoming personnel to report to their designated stations to complete paperwork.

Medical was the most important, but, luckily, took the least amount of time to process. I started making my way to the exit signs of the gym. My intent was to leave completely unnoticed. I worked my way around the hugging family members with tears of joy on their faces and made it to the desk where I would be able to sign out.

Once I got there, the sergeant said not all officers had to go through this process, so I was free to leave. As soon as I walked out, I saw a taxi dropping off a tardy family. I quickly grabbed the cab and said, "Hale Koa Hotel, please."

* * *

I arrived at the hotel later that night, exhausted wanting nothing more than to down a killer Mai Tai by the pool. I didn't want to talk to anyone or be seen by anyone I knew. I just wanted to have a drink and fall into bed. I ordered a Mai Tai, immediately followed by another, then another.

At this point I was feeling tired but more social and the bar was beginning to get crowded. Drinking three Mai Tai's in quick succession really pushed me over the edge. I could really tell they were doing the trick because I found myself making more and more small talk with other hotel guests, as though the last few bloody months in Iraq had never happened, almost as if everything was normal. As if I were normal. It was all so surreal.

I woke up the following day butt naked on my hotel room bed. Like they say in the Army, that's never a good thing, especially if you wake up with a quarter in your hand (the implication being that someone had their way with you and only paid a quarter for the experience).

I did not wake up with a quarter in my hand, so at least I had that going for me.

I got out of bed slowly because my head was still in a fog and the room would spin when I closed my eyes— a clear sign that I'd had too much to drink the night before. The minibar in my room was stocked with cold bottled water that was being offered for an obscene amount of money, but I didn't care about the cost.

My head felt like it was going to explode. I went downstairs to the hotel convenience store in my sleeping shorts and a tank top and got some Tylenol. The moment I left my room, maids went quickly to work cleaning, so I decided to go to the restaurant and get some breakfast.

I still had not contacted my kids or wife. It's hard to describe how broken down the line of communication becomes with your family once your PTSD-influenced behavior has wrought so much damage. The loving person who went to war comes back an angry, withdrawn, short-fused, couch potato with an affinity for drinking, drugs, porn, or all of the above.

Every time you reach out to your family to try to smooth things over, it's like you're testing the emotional waters, because you just do not know how deep the wounds will be on the other end of the line or what you will be made to answer for. In the end, when you finally decide to call, you do so with such trepidation that ultimately you start avoiding it altogether, until you finally get to the point where it's easier not to communicate at all rather than to continually attempt to navigate such treacherous waters over and over.

As these thoughts bounced around the inside of my hungover head, I flipped through the real estate section of the local paper and spotted an ad for a two-bedroom rental overlooking Sharks Cove in Pupukea' on the North Shore. The thought of being deployed again was vastly more appealing than returning to San Antonio to face my family. I simply did not feel worthy of them, and they sure as hell did not deserve my crazy ass. My best bet was to stay put here in Hawaii.

I decided to check out the apartment as soon as possible, knowing all too well that sometimes getting deployed again could take several months, and it would require signing a waiver for my dwell time.

The clock started on dwell time the minute you got back home and, technically, the Army could not touch you for a year, but of course the Army always found ways to get around that rule.

In my case I was more than happy to sign a waiver so I could get out of there as quickly as possible. The apartment was off the beaten path on the North Shore. The only noteworthy thing about it was that they were filming the show "Lost" across the street, but that was fine with me. I wasn't looking to socialize. When I wasn't working, I avoided people as much as possible and prided myself on not speaking to a soul for entire weekends. My only focus was to secure another deployment, so I could put myself in harm's way once again, and hopefully not come back alive.

CHAPTER 9

SUBTLE AND POWERFUL

2008, AFRICA

IT WASN'T LONG BEFORE MY wish came true. Within six months of my return from Iraq, I was deployed once again. As luck would have it, the only thing available was an assignment with a Special Forces group in Africa and it turned out to be a nice break. I wasn't home, so I didn't have to deal with my impending divorce. Communication was very poor in Africa, so even if I'd wanted to talk with people back home, it wasn't possible. I was essentially on cruise control.

I volunteered at the clinic on base, but when I was out on a mission, I was gone for weeks and even months at a time. Like all Special Operation Missions, the work we did in Africa is classified, but I will say that I was able to see a lot of countries, some of which were recruiting stations for Al-Qaeda, Al Shabbah, or rift valley rebels responsible for unspeakable atrocities.

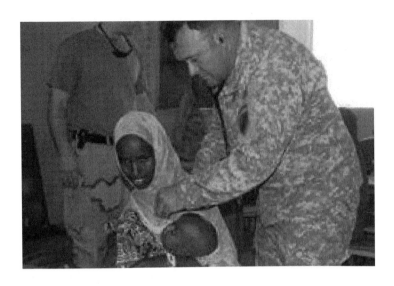

CONDUCTING A MEDICAL CIVIL ACTION PROGRAM (MEDCAP) IN MILO, ETHIOPIA.

Wherever we went, we stuck out like sore thumbs, because we were the only "Muzungu" (Swahili for white people) around. It wasn't like being in South America or Europe, where we could hide or blend in.

Not all of our work was classified, however. Some of our time in Africa was spent performing humanitarian work, and as a French linguist, I was able to communicate in the various francophone countries we visited as we traveled around the continent. We were based out of Djibouti but traveled to Ethiopia, Kenya, Tanzania, Uganda, Democratic Republic of Congo, the Seychelles and Madagascar, to name a few.

My time in Africa virtually flew by until the last few months, when I had the opportunity to take a long pass and go to Tanzania to climb Mount Kilimanjaro. I remember watching "The Snows of Kilimanjaro," this a short story by Ernest Hemingmay, that captured my imagination as a child. I had a goal and that was to climb Kilimajaro and fly the U.S flag for the men and women who never made it home from Iraq or Afghanistan. This long journey and sacrifice would be in their honor.

I flew from Djibouti to Ethiopia and then Arusha, Tanzania. I had pre-arranged a team through a guide company several months prior and had the good fortune of getting Morris, a third generation Kilimanjaro guide who had about 300 summits under his belt.

The plan was to meet up at a hotel and when I arrived Morris was already waiting for me in the garden. We greeted one another, ordered some drinks and discussed the plan for the ascent to the summit. Morris spoke softly but with purpose and had a way about him that made you stop and listen. I took to him immediately. Not only was he the spitting image of hip-hop artist Mos Def, but he was extremely knowledgeable and seemed to genuinely care for his team.

The following day we made it to the entrance of the park, and Morris had me open my duffle bags for inspection. As he rifled through my bags, he took out any items that would be of no use to us and tossed them all into a box off to the side. I felt like a rookie recruit.

POSING FOR A PICTURE ALONG THE MARANGU ROUTE TO KILIMANJARO.

Once he'd finished paring down my belongings, he turned to me and said, "Mr. Marc, are you ready to climb to the ceiling of Africa?"

I nodded.

He smiled and said, "Let's go. We have a four-hour hike to first camp."

As soon as the words left his mouth, three porters who were carrying our supplies ran up ahead of us, singing as they went. Their job was to arrive at camp two hours ahead of us to set up and cook dinner.

As we watched them go, Morris leaned in and said, "Mr. Marc remember this: If I say 'pole pole' it means slow down. It is very important to slowly climb Kili. You do not want to have to leave because you get sick. Don't worry, I teach you everything and I help you get to Uhuru peak."

I smiled and thanked him.

* * *

On day three of our ascent, the air was thinner and it was more difficult to maintain a steady pace. My feet were killing me but not badly enough for me to want to turn around. I was driven to complete this mission the same way I'd been trained to complete any mission I set out on as a soldier in the Army. However, this mission was additionally fueled by my desire not to let down my fallen brothers and sisters. I could not bear being another disappointment to myself.

Morris handed me a pill to prevent altitude sickness and said: "Take this now, and tonight before we climb further I will give you another one". He knew the drill for preventing altitude sickness well. Although he had no need for the meds himself, he knew exactly when a dose was needed based on the experience of 300 climbs.

At this point I was tired and sore but not yet feeling the effects of altitude sickness. I feared the worst was yet to come. The climb to the summit was not until very early in the morning and the temperature at Kibo Huts was already about 30 degrees cooler than it had been at base camp.

KILIMANJARO NATIONAL PARK

We arrived at Kibo Huts at 4 p.m. and Morris quickly ensured that I had a bed and a warm meal. As usual, the food was very satisfying--a nice bowl of leek soup and pasta with vegetables. I was also served hot tea and scones.

"Mr. Marc you need to sleep now," Morris said after I'd finished eating. "I will wake you up at midnight and we will then climb to Gilman's Point."

It was still early so I walked outside the worn-down wooden structure that would house us for the evening and looked up, tilting my head all the way back so I could see the top of the peak he was referring to. "Shit," I thought to myself. "That is way the hell up there and that is not even Uhuru peak."

That night, I slept as well as one can in an open bay with both men and women sharing living space and, luckily, the noise of arriving climbers didn't bother me at all. I got some well-needed rest.

I was awakened at 11:30 p.m. and told to get ready because we were leaving at midnight. Morris had coffee and cookies waiting for me and had already prepared our canteens and filled our camelbacks with fresh water. I was excited but also nervous. I did not want to fail on this mission. I needed to summit Uhuru peak for many personal reasons, but above them all was my desire to fly the American flag in memory of all the fallen men and women who died in combat in both Iraq and Afghanistan. I hadn't made it this far to give up now.

However, altitude sickness was a very real danger at this point. Morris gave me another pill in hopes of averting any problems on the ascent. Bruce Springsteen's ballad "Should I Fall Behind" kept playing in my head and I kept repeating the lyrics to myself as we left Kibo huts.

We started our ascent at almost midnight following Switchback Trail "pole pole" all the way up the side of the glacier. Footing was not guaranteed as the path beneath our feet consisted of small loose gravel. We stopped every hour to rest, and as I sat there gasping for air, Morris calmly smoked a cigarette. About halfway up I tried drinking out of my camelback but nothing would come out The hose was frozen solid. Luckily I had a bottle of water in my rucksack that was not quite frozen.

MOUNT KILIMANJARO

We finally arrived to Gilman's Point. This was only the first summit and I could hear my lungs rattling a bit, but I needed to continue. I kept telling myself I couldn't let all those souls down. However, when I look back, I realize my real motivation was a desperate need to talk to God. I wanted to ask Him for forgiveness. I figured if He couldn't hear me at 20,000 feet, He never would.

Despite the fact that I'd started losing faith in God several years prior when I could no longer face myself in the mirror, my spirituality remained an important part of who I was. I'd broken away from the church out of guilt and because divorce was not allowed. I figured I was damned to hell anyway, because my incompetence had prevented me from saving the lives of my fellow soldiers in combat.

In my mind, I should have studied harder or somehow tried harder. Instead, they had died and now I carried this overwhelming guilt and pain in my heart. My soul was plagued with fear, regret, shame, helplessness and hopelessness. I was not worthy of a prayer or a life but I needed to seek God's forgiveness and ask Him for guidance on how I could atone for my sins.

Perhaps my prayers didn't deserve to be heard, but I wasn't giving up until I'd tried.

* * *

After a five hour climb to Gilman's point we rested for about twenty minutes or the time it took Morris to smoke two cigarets. Mo got up and we slowly made our way around the glacier to Uhuru Peak. I followed a short distance behind him, tired and taking short breaths but determined to succeed. My lungs were full of fluid and sounded awful. The blowing wind was frigid and the snow made the trail harder to navigate, not to mention that my feet were now completely numb. I did not care. I was going to make it to the second summit. We arrived at Uhuru Peak about an hour after summiting Gilman's Point. There was not much there other than a sign that read "Uhuru Peak, Tanzania. You are at the highest point in Africa. Elevation 5895 meters above sea level"(19,340 feet). Morris congratulated me on achieving something very few people in the world have accomplished. I had already explained to Morris my intent and reasoning for climbing Kili, so he understood how important this was to me above and beyond physical endurance.

FLYING THE US FLAG ON TOP OF MOUNT KILIMANJARO IN MEMORY OF MY FALLEN BROTHERS AND SISTERS DURING OPERATION IRAQI FREEDOM AND OPERATION ENDURING FREEDOM.

This was a conversation we'd had long before we got there. I asked him kindly to take a picture of me by the sign as both my cameras were frozen solid and the only thing I had left with which to capture this moment was my iPhone. I pulled out my flag and carefully and respectfully unfolded it.

"I am so sorry I could not save you," I said. "I will always carry you guys in my heart."

I said this out loud almost yelling with full emotion. I think poor Morris looked over his shoulder to see who I was talking to.

I also asked God for forgiveness, but the only thing I got in return was the smell of Morris' cigarette, as smoke filled the air around us. I felt cheated, sad, and foolish to think God would have given me a sign. I sat down on a rock facing Mount Kenya and quietly began to fold up my flag.

"You know it is almost time," Morris said.
"For what?" I asked.
"You will see Mr. Marc," he said.

I kept folding my flag until it was the shape of a perfect triangle. I sat there broken, heavy-hearted and wanting so badly to be dead and forgotten. I placed the flag back into my backpack and attempted to break up the ice that had formed on the hose of my camelback with little success.

I felt Morris lean in.
"Now Mr. Marc," he whispered.

AHEAD MOUNT KENYA AND BEYOND THAT THE DAWN OF AFRICA

The wind slowed down and there was an odd silence. I looked up toward the horizon and saw the most beautiful thing I have ever seen: Africa waking up. The sun rose from the ground, bigger and closer than I have ever see it. The sky was an amazing purple-blue with orange, red, yellows and pinks mixed in. I stood there witnessing an unparalleled beauty.

Below, I could see clouds moving slowly. I saw birds flying in formation. I looked up and there was the sun again. It was amazing to see this dramatic birth of a day. The sun warmed my face. No longer were my feet hurting.

I finally felt God touch me with the warmth of the sun. I asked again for forgiveness. I told him how heavy my heart was and how much I missed my soul. I found myself crying with relief. Tears were streaming down my face, as I stood there in the presence of such beauty.

There were so many feelings just pouring out. I could hardly control my emotions. To this day, I still wonder if there was a moment there where God Himself was there with me.

The sun rose higher in the sky and I realized I had just witnessed the first day of my healing. All along God had been there with me on my journey, but I'd never understood that, because I was so focused on wanting to die. To this day I am not a religious person and I am still fairly sure I am going straight to hell, but on that day I was in the presence of something immensely powerful, yet subtle. Had I not taken a few moments to sit and realize what was happening I would have missed it.

Morris finally asked if I was ok.

"I will be," I said.

CHAPTER 10

SONJA THE CATALYST

WHEN I FIRST MET MARC, he had just returned from a year-long deployment and had recently gone through a very ugly divorce after years of being separated. He was blamed for the decay of the marriage by both his ex-wife and his two older daughters and felt that he'd been tossed aside like a piece of garbage. All these negative emotions paired with his PTSD symptoms made him feel increasingly suicidal. He had not been shown love for many years nor did he feel worthy of love. His self-esteem was in shreds and he was barely hanging on.

He could not comprehend what I saw in him when we first started dating. It was incredibly hard for him to see himself through my eyes. From my perspective, he was a strong man who had survived hell and thrived. I saw an incredibly intelligent man who had been around the world, spoke five languages fluently, and was successful in building three very challenging careers for himself. I saw a generous man with a great big heart who took meticulous care of his children and patients, but who was suffering emotionally.

We had several conversations where he referred to himself as tossed away garbage and that was how he truly felt about himself. The guilt trips he received from his ex-wife paired with the guilt he carried from not being able to save every single soldier while deployed was eating him alive.

The first time I spent the night, it was apparent that he had some problems. The first thing I noticed was that he never slept. Since he didn't sleep, I didn't sleep when I was with him, and that was almost all of the time. He would go to bed early—around 9 or 10 PM—and by midnight he was either wide awake pacing in the living room, or tossing and turning from horrible nightmares.

The nightmares were almost nightly and occurred multiple times a night. I knew when he was having them because his breathing became more rapid and shallow, and it sounded almost like he could not catch his breath. He would then start thrashing around, and by the time I woke him he would be sobbing and hyperventilating. Frequently he would mutter out loud about the eyes of one of his soldiers staring at him with accusations because he'd been unable to save him.

The worst part for me was bearing witness to his pain. It was torture to see him in that much agony day in and day out. I still only know a small fraction about the horrendous images that plague him, but even with that limited knowledge, the common themes are survivor's guilt, shame and feeling unworthy of life. No credit is taken for the many lives he saved nor the awesome care he gave to the wounded and injured, only self-flagellation for those he couldn't save and for the families who are no longer whole.

The other thing I noticed shortly after meeting Marc was that he lived in a state of constant anxiety and paranoia. In a nanosecond all of his thoughts would spin out of control like a tornado and quickly devolve into a worst-case scenario.

If he got an email from his boss, it meant he was getting fired or someone had made a complaint against him. If I did not call when I'd said I would, or if I changed plans at the last minute, it meant I was doing something I should not be doing or that I was going to leave him and find someone more worthy/intelligent/attractive.

Despite being one of the most well-respected clinicians on base and being involved in a loving and stable relationship, he remained suspicious of everything and everyone. No matter what, he saw monsters coming toward him and it was emotionally and physically draining for me to consistently be in the position of talking him off of a ledge.

It wasn't long before I devised ways to calm him down. I found that deep breathing exercises worked best for calming him down, allowing him to refocus his thoughts toward what was actually happening rather than what he was imagining was happening. There were several times when I just wanted to indulge in a good adolescent eye-roll when he began to panic over nothing, but for him the panic was real and any show of disregard for this feelings on my part only would have succeeded in pushing him away. Honor, loyalty and respect were definitely key to my honey feeling like he could continue to trust and confide in me.

Marc also engaged in a lot of avoidant behaviors, and I started to catch myself indulging in the same patterns. My whole lifestyle changed. He didn't go shopping when stores were crowded and avoided loud noises, so we only shopped late at night on weekdays, and I trained myself to become more vigilant about my surroundings.

Movies were selected based on which were the least likely to cause a reaction from Marc, and celebrations were only attended if they didn't include fireworks. Date nights were outings to low-key restaurants rather than packed nightclubs or bars. I am a total dancer girl and I used to love to go salsa dancing three or four times a week, but once I met Marc I completely stopped. Nightclubs made him feel very insecure and overwhelmed.

I still vividly remember the Friday night we went to an expensive restaurant in Waikiki to celebrate a special occasion. It was right after we began dating so I hadn't yet seen Marc's reaction to fireworks. We had just ordered our meal, were sipping our wine, laughing, eating our appetizer and enjoying the romantic atmosphere. Then the fireworks began. I love fireworks, but the instant they started, Marc's face drained of all color and he turned a horrible shade of green. I thought for sure he was going to dive underneath the table.

The fireworks only lasted for about five minutes, but those were the longest five minutes of our lives and completely ruined our dinner. Even after they were over Marc couldn't refocus. The damage was done. He might as well have been eating cardboard instead of a fancy steak dinner, and I felt terrible for failing to foresee that the fireworks would cause this reaction in him.

I had lived in Hawaii for years and knew about the weekly fireworks and, as a psychologist, I should have known what a big trigger they would be. Of course at the time, I was just thinking about enjoying a romantic evening with the man I was falling in love with and did not think about any outside factors since I had never dated anyone with severe PTSD. Needless to say, we never again returned to Waikiki on a Friday night.

Even worse than going out and risking a traumatic reaction, though, were the times when I had to leave Marc home alone. As a Behavioral Health Officer in the Hawaii Army National Guard, I would be gone for 10 to 12 hours at a time on drill weekends, and, if we were in the field, I would be gone from Friday evening until Sunday evening. By the time I'd return home, Marc would be severely depressed, often reiterating his thoughts of being worthless. My worst fear was that I would one day return home to find him dead.

The more I altered my lifestyle, the more noticeable the changes became to those around me and friends began to express concern. One of my girlfriends had been married to someone in the Navy so she had some experience with dating somebody in the military, but for the most part Marc didn't want anybody to know about his PTSD so I wasn't sharing details of our life together. He would have felt betrayed had I talked about it too much. I felt very, very isolated.

* * *

About three months into our relationship, I started broaching the topic of treatment with Marc. As part of my professional development, I'd been attending training with Edna Foa, an Israeli professor of clinical psychology, and she was speaking to us about prolonged exposure as a way to treat PTSD.

It was a four-day training and every day I was coming home, excited about it and telling Marc, 'You gotta do this! You need this!" He definitely was not excited so I brought out my packet and showed him the data. He is a Physician Assistant so it helped that I had clinical evidence and could prove this was not just hocus-pocus. This was the No. 1 treatment for his condition.

He was pretty reluctant to engage in treatment. He'd already had a bad experience with a psychiatrist and he was worried about other soldiers judging him for being in treatment. He also thought that by seeking help I would somehow think less of him, when in reality I understood how much courage it took. The one thing he kept coming back to, however, was that he didn't want to go through another divorce. He wasn't sure he would survive another bad break up. He kept saying 'I want to be better for you.'

It made me happy and sad at the same time. I wanted him to want to be better for himself, because he deserved it, and not just to make me happy.

I thought I was fully prepared for outpatient treatment. It was only going to be once a week and as a therapist I knew exactly what to expect. In my own naïve way, I assumed that since I had conducted therapy sessions myself, I could weather the storm much more easily than spouses and partners who had never experienced therapy themselves, professionally or personally. We'd been through so much already that I figured it couldn't get much worse.

At least that's what I kept telling myself. Little did I know that conducting therapy is far easier than being a patient or being romantically involved with a patient going through treatment. It can get a lot worse. And it did.

The first few individual sessions were particularly painful because the intensity of Marc's PTSD symptoms increased immediately following each session. Marc's treatments took place every Wednesday at 15:00 and the idea was that he would have time at home to reflect and recover after his sessions before I got home from work.

In reality, however, I cut out of work at exactly 16:30 to drive him home. Each time he'd have a nearly visible black cloud over his head, reacting in anger to anything I said or asked. I tried to be his cheerleader but it was brutal. Those sessions really shook him up.

He'd had it. Anything I said or did could go in a negative direction. I was trying to be Suzy Sunshine and put in a lot of positivity but I felt like I was walking on eggshells, and I was frequently blamed for convincing him to seek treatment in the first place.

Even more excruciating, though, was when Marc went to bed. Wednesdays and Thursdays were loaded with nightmares that began within minutes of Marc falling asleep and it would take up to 30 minutes to calm him down. We went through this about two to three times a night, each time with me coaching him through deep breathing exercises while rubbing his arm and assuring him that everything was okay.

I went from being the type of heavy sleeper who could sleep through an earthquake or a tornado (and, yes, I have done both) to sleeping so lightly that I was attuned to the slightest fluctuation in Marc's breathing pattern. By the time the weekend rolled around we were both exhausted and Marc would repeatedly reiterate that he didn't want to return to treatment. I felt like the worst kind of scum for making him continue treatment despite cognitively understanding that he needed therapy in order to heal. There was a huge part of me that wanted to throw in the towel and revert to engaging in avoidance behavior with him.

The focus was entirely on Marc with no attention paid to the toll all of this took on me and his children, and no thought was given to how Marc's PTSD affected my work and my quality of life. But it did. I didn't sleep on Wednesdays or Thursdays then I would go into the field for the weekend starting at 5:30 on Friday. By the time my shift ended on Sunday night, I'd worked seven days straight, then I'd race home as fast as I could to make sure Marc was still alive.

Suicide was a huge risk factor. My anxiety was high, I wasn't eating healthy food and I was so exhausted I started getting sick all of the time. Ultimately I started taking off of work on Monday or Tuesday following drill weekends just so I could recover.

I was drained of both physical and emotional resources and I had no place to go for help. I was all alone. I was not a spouse so I wasn't eligible for military benefits; I was the only Behavioral Health Officer in the Army Guard, so I had no professional peers; and the majority of my friends were civilians, so they couldn't relate to what I was going through. The few times the topic came up, I felt like any discussion of my life would be betraying Marc, so I started to just pretend everything was fine instead of going into details.

When his anger flared up, it was very scary. One time he became upset with his mother over something minor and he lit into her with a fury I had not seen prior. His behavior was so vile it made me second-guess our relationship. He was almost like the Hulk. Through it all, though, I was able to see the wounded man beneath the anger and that man has always been worthy of my love and attention.

Dating Marc was a lot more to take on than I ever could have imagined it would be. He needed more caregiving, reassurance and love than I have ever given in any relationship. That first year of our relationship was so exhausting I wasn't so sure we'd make it. In the end, I am grateful for having stuck by him. He has become a wonderful husband and father and I can't imagine life without him.

* * *

Piece by piece, our life has come back together. It is still a work in progress but I rarely see anger or avoidance these days. Marc is much calmer, more relaxed and loving toward his family and friends.

One of our biggest milestones came in 2013 when we went to Disneyland together for New Year's. In spite of the crowds, we enjoyed ourselves and Marc even loved the evening water show with all the noise and fireworks that came along with it. That was tremendous—I expected a large meltdown from him.

The best decision we ever made, though, was adopting our dog Douglas. From the moment we brought him home, Marc's mood finally changed for the better. That pitbull does whatever Marc is doing so when I have to be gone for long periods of time, Marc has Douglas to keep him company. Thank God.

CHAPTER 11

MORE THERAPY

AT THIS POINT I HAD been on medication for about 6 months or so. Prior to heading to Africa, I'd decided to get back on medication in the hopes of offsetting the side effects of Mefloquine, an anti-malaria medicine. The side effects of Mefloquine are either awesome or fucked up because Mefloquin gives you very vivid dreams. In my case, they're mostly fucked up.

Despite my best efforts, I was still waking up in the middle of the night to check every door and window, only to end up sitting on the couch dead tired but too afraid to sleep. This went on for several months. Sonja, who at the time was still my girlfriend, as we hadn't yet gotten married, approached the topic with a lot of wisdom and tact.

"You are an amazing person," she told me. "And you deserve to be happy and free of whatever it is that is keeping you from being the best you can be."

With those words something snapped in my head. In that very instant what she was saying finally registered in my mind. Life is funny that way. Sometimes in a split second everything changes. The way we feel about something or someone is a good example, like when you realize your marriage is over. It's a moment of complete clarity, and then you just know.

After that, I made the decision to at least try therapy again in order to get well. I wanted to be better for her. We'd just started dating, but somehow I knew it would end up being more. I knew it was time to put away all my hang ups and fears and just go for it, so I could finally cross that abyss and be on the path toward healing. I'll admit I was still resistant about sharing my deepest thoughts with someone, especially since my first experience with counseling had been horrible to say the least. But, I wanted to be a little more whole, slightly less broken, and a bit more forgiven.

SCHOFIELD BARRACKS, HAWAII 2009

It was a dark day in Hawaii. The skies had been promising rain all day. I waited almost until the end of the workday. Only one more thing to do, and that was to meet with my social worker. It all seemed very reminiscent of the first time I'd met with a therapist.

This would be my second counselor and I was nervous about his bedside manner since the first counselor's had completely sucked. The first time around I'd done a lot of research and picked the guy who seemed to be the most qualified, yet turned out to be a complete douche bag. This time around Sonja found a guy who she thought would be a good match. Off I went.

Once again, I found myself sitting in a room next to mostly lower enlisted soldiers who gave me funny looks while I sat there playing bejeweled on my phone as I waited. Surely they were wondering why there was a major sitting among them wearing a clinic badge. They probably assumed I was waiting for some professional advice about a patient or something. Of course my cover was blown when my counselor came out and called my name.

I looked up and in front of me stood a tall young man who spoke softly and confidently and looked to be of southern European and Asian descent. He looked a little bit like a more awkward version of Keanu Reeves, truth be told. As we walked down to his office, he attempted to engage me in small talk. I never know how to respond to that kind of pleasantry. My first instinct is to be either funny or sarcastic, so I didn't engage in much conversation. Besides, I was too busy being hyper observant, as I took everything in, attempting to assess just exactly who this person was.

My new counselor was one of those people who has the natural ability to calm people down simply by using a soothing tone of voice. He asked me to have a seat and went over everything in my file thoroughly, asking a lot of questions while making appropriate eye contact. Never once did he turn his back to me or check his watch for the time, like the first counselor I'd met with.

This doctor (we'll call him Dr. Reeves) seemed genuinely eager to help me. I found myself liking him right from the beginning. His ability to ask questions in a non-threatening manner showed he was a seasoned and compassionate professional. After all, the guy was willing to spend 90 minutes per session with victims of PTSD instead of the standard 45. He purposely set aside the extra time, knowing our treatment would be extensive.

Because he was a civilian, he immediately disclosed to me that he'd never been in combat. That kind of honesty was reassuring to me and a clear indication that he either had excellent insight or had worked with enough soldiers to understand our need to feel like we were talking to someone who understood what we'd been through.

After that, I made up my mind that he was someone who could help me. I was going to share with him all that troubled me. On my way out of his office that day, we set up 90-minute sessions for every Wednesday for the entire coming year. I had no idea what to expect since I'd never had treatment—only drugs—and I never could have guessed what I would eventually go through. All I knew was that I wanted to be better. Even though I was still a little leery about everything, I committed to the process once and for all.

After the initial get-to-know-you phase, it was decided that my treatment would consist of long-term exposure therapy or Eye Movement Desensitization Reprocessing (EMDR). Both modalities were provoking with the goal of returning me to the experiences that I couldn't shake. We started first with Prolonged Exposure, a methodology that helps you overcome painful memories by revisiting them multiple times during a session so that ultimately you become desensitized to the trauma over a period of time.

It's a lot like the treatments used to cure a food or drug allergy in which the doctor starts off administering small harmless doses of whatever it is that is causing the allergic reaction with the expectation that the Patient will start developing a resistance to the allergen.

In my case there were countless scenarios playing in my head from my days in Desert Storm, Kosovo, and Operation Iraqi Freedom. To tackle ALL of these memories was not necessarily as important as addressing the common denominators in these scenarios that were causing my ongoing suffering.

The hardest part of this process for me was discerning between things that upset me (ie: blatant disrespect or somebody making snap judgements about me based on nothing more than the fact that I have tattoos) versus those that were merely annoying such as people who love to one-up others in daily conversation (in my early days of PTSD that would have been enough to completely set me off).

I did finally manage to dredge up the three or four things that stuck out the most, and I focused on those—that seemed to be more effective. The other stuff bothered me, but somehow addressing the big issues made the lesser annoyances seem not nearly as bad.

Of course, there were days when I swore I wouldn't go back for the next session. You grow tired of it; you hit a plateau. But, like I said, I was committed to the process at this point. From the very first session when the doctor suggested we talk about the four or five things that bothered me, I was vested. I was going to do this and it was on like Donkey Kong.

CHAPTER 12

TREATMENT

PROLONGED EXPOSURE WAS NOT AS intense as EMDR, but it was still very hard to take. I would sit there and go over scenarios in my head while Dr. Reeves listened patiently through my tears and sorrow. It took a little bit to open up at first, but my mind was made up, and I wanted to get well. More importantly, I needed to move on and let go.

As I told my story, tears flowed, and all the demons that lived inside me slowly emerged. I remember Dr. Reeves sitting there looking at me not with judgment or pity, but only concern. When the first session ended, he handed me a CD with a recording of our consultation and said in a calm voice, "Major, you have some homework to do. I will see you next Wednesday."

As I exited his office, he gave me that smile people give you when you board an elevator, the tightening of the lips stretched across teeth as if to show empathy without conveying too much emotion. When I got home later that day, my head swirled as thoughts and emotions I'd formerly suppressed began bubbling to the surface.

As the weeks went on, Wednesdays became more and more difficult. Talking about things you have never shared with another living soul is more difficult than you can imagine. Reliving terrifying moments over and over is almost too much to bear. But, with time, I got better and better at sharing my stories. It took about four to six weeks of painful Prolonged Exposure therapy before I peaked and started to level off a little, but therapy did not end after that 90-minute session each week.

My work continued at home when I listened to the CDs my counselor handed me every Wednesday. I was supposed to listen to the CD multiple times before returning the following week in an effort to desensitize me to the memories that continued to haunt me.

To hear my recorded voice telling one particular story about 17 times over and over nearly broke me. It was Christmas Day 2003 in Iraq, and I was sitting in my sleeping area. The small room, which ultimately led to a corridor, had mildewed walls that gave off the odor of wet clothing forgotten in a washer for several days. The corridor outside the room led to another similar room, and then finally to our triage area where we would evaluate our wounded and determine how to prioritize them.

That day, a medic knocked on my door and yelled, "Sir, Incoming!" Now, the word incoming had two meanings in Iraq: Either a helicopter of wounded was landing, and we needed to attend to them, or there were incoming mortars, and we needed to seek shelter. I immediately ran to the trauma room.

When I got there they were bringing in a soldier who was burned on more than 80% of his body surface. He had two IV lines in him, and his vitals were being closely monitored, especially his breathing and airway. I stood next to the bed to help with the management of this injured soldier when, out of nowhere, a hand grabbed mine and he said, "Please tell my wife that I love her."

I didn't know what to say. At this point, I knew in my heart he probably wasn't going to make it to Baghdad for further treatment much less the hospital on base in Germany. Then they told me how he got burned. His convoy had been held up secondary to a road-side bomb. The soldier began pulling other soldiers from burning vehicles to save them. Disregarding his own safety by trying to save his fellow soldiers and eventually burning himself to his demise.

My boss handed me a satellite phone and said, "Please dial his home number."

I looked at him with confusion, because I was still holding on to hope that the soldier might make it out alive. My boss just gave me a nod.

It was then that I realized that my initial gut reaction was probably more accurate—this soldier wasn't likely to make it much further. I handed him the phone so he could talk to his wife, thinking it would probably be the last time he did so. After he hung up, we dressed his wounds and got him to Baghdad. I have no idea what happened to him after that.

Part two of that story happened later that day when soldiers came to me to ask if he was going to be OK. In order to keep a positive vibe going, I downplayed the severity of the burned soldier's injuries and told them he was going to be just fine. I did this, because I did not feel it was right for me to take away the only thing that they were hanging on to, and that was hope. Their eyes met mine, and in that moment they looked at me with resentment and reproach, as if I'd done something wrong, and I was to blame for what had happened.

That story is one that still chokes me up, even as proof that this course of therapy was effective. In fact, by the end of that year, I finally began to see a light at the end of the tunnel. This was a huge breakthrough for me, because for the longest time I didn't believe that such a light existed.

CHAPTER 13

DOUGLAS: MAN'S BEST FRIEND

Douglas #2

NORTH SHORE, OAHU 2010

DURING THE SAME YEAR THAT I was having breakthroughs in therapy, I experienced another major milestone in my PTSD journey. I had reached the realization that I needed companionship. Up until that point, I'd just wanted to be left alone. Living on the North Shore was very lonely and isolating and now that I was opening up more and more, it was starting to get to me. I remembered reading an article that said people who have pets are less likely to commit suicide, and that stayed in my mind. I had been looking to adopt a dog for a while, and now I was finally ready to take on the responsibility of caring for another living being.

I knew the dog had to come from the pound, because that's where all dogs that are thrown away end up, and I felt I'd also been discarded. I wanted a dog that nobody would ever adopt. I wanted a dog with sad eyes, and a great big heart that would accept my love.

I also wanted to include my new girlfriend in this decision, to share with her these good feelings of hope and progress that I was feeling. So, together, we went down to the pound dog shelter in Kapolei on the west side of Oahu. It took me about an hour to get there from the North Shore but that was OK, since I really wanted to think about the kind of dog I wanted to adopt.

I knew I was looking for something like a pit bull or similar breed, and I knew I had a good chance of finding one since Hawaii is such a bully breed-friendly state. On one hand, I wanted to keep an open mind in case I didn't find the dog I pictured in my mind, but on the other hand, my mind was already made up. I wasn't going to settle for the sake of adopting just any old pet—I wanted a pit bull.

We arrived at the shelter and Sonja jumped right out of the Jeep, making a beeline for the entrance. I think she was more excited about finding a pet for me than I was. She was all about the puppies and kittens of the annoying variety (ie: small fluffy balls of fur you can fit into a purse), so I found myself wondering whether bringing her had been a mistake.

As it turned out, it didn't really matter. Our first visit turned out to be a wasted trip anyway. We looked and looked for just the right dog, but no luck. They had tons of puppies that were very cute, but I wanted an adult dog, so we decided to wait a bit longer and continue searching.

* * *

Three weeks later I asked my girlfriend if she wanted to come along with me and see if we had better luck. She was elated that I'd again asked her to come with me. (Truth be told, I probably couldn't have stopped her from coming with me, whether I'd invited her or not. She's small, but once her mind is set, I have very little chance of changing it!) She quickly jumped into the Jeep and we headed back to the shelter.

The shelter was an old warehouse the Navy had offered up to be used as a no-kill center for dogs and cats, and they were fairly successful in finding homes for their animals. This time around we really took our time. I sat with several dogs, but none of them really did it for me. None of them were solid-looking enough. I wanted a real bruiser.

We worked our way toward the back of the warehouse, and

as we approached the last kennel, a dog named Ace caught our attention, mainly because he was sitting in the oddest position. He was kneeling on his hind legs so that they pointed backward as if he was getting ready to do a "girl"-style push up. He looked up at me with his huge head and opened his mouth revealing missing teeth. His face and nose bore the scars of having been mistreated by abusive owners. As he closed his mouth, you could see the smile of the pit bull in him. I asked the attendant about him.

"The only thing I know about this one is that he was brought in late last night from one of the other shelters on the island," she said.

I asked her if it would be okay to get into the cage with him. She didn't seem to think that was an odd request, so I walked into the kennel where I could see him much better. He was a beautiful dog that had been treated like shit for a very long time. Ace sat alone in his kennel waiting for someone to adopt him.

It was then that I realized how similar we were. We'd both been thrown away and we were both prisoners. His kennel was his prison and mine was a life lived in the shadow of fear, distrust, guilt, and anger. We sat together in his kennel for a while in silence. I said nothing. Ace got up and walked around me, casually sizing me up. He was looking at me but wasn't committing to fully engaging with me. I sat alone for several minutes, until he came and bumped me with his huge head. Finally he sat next to me and leaned on me. I knew instantly that I had found my dog and that his new name would be Douglas.

Several years back I'd lived in California and gone to a shelter and adopted another pit bull named Douglas. Or at least I thought I had. I'd had the dog no more than two weeks when the shelter called to tell me they'd accidentally given me a dog that had been brought in for temporary boarding—not adoption. Obviously when the owners returned from vacation to claim their dog they were surprised to find out he'd been given away and they wanted their pet back. I returned him reluctantly and decided the next pit bull I owned would be named Douglas in his memory.

Douglas No. 2 and I sat there for several more minutes while Sonja spoke animatedly with the attendant. She was excited to see me overjoyed at having found the dog I'd been searching for. And, because she's so organized, she was able to get all the information and pay the required adoption fees quickly so that everything was set by the time I got to the front desk of the shelter.

Before we finalized the adoption, Sonja had only one request, and that was to see how Douglas got along with cats. Part of the deal with her was, if I loved her, I would have to love her cranky ass cat as well. So the attendant walked Douglas through the cat cages to test his temperament, and Douglas walked right by them as if he didn't care. In fact, he basically ignored them and walked right out. Douglas had passed the cat test with flying colors. We were good to go.

The manager of the animal shelter told me that I could not take Douglas home that day, but that I could return to pick him up over the weekend once he was cleared by the veterinarian. I really didn't want to leave him at the shelter. It was only Monday, and I'd have to wait a whole week before seeing him again.

* * *

Saturday finally came, and I returned to the shelter at about ten in the morning. There were already a dozen cars in front of the shelter when I arrived. After my first disappointing attempt, I was a little paranoid something would happen to screw up this adoption. I started to worry that they'd given Douglas away to someone else. As I walked into the shelter there were several families touring the facility. Being around so many people in such tight quarters was making me feel even more anxious. I started practicing the breathing exercises I'd been taught in therapy in order to calm myself down.

The lady behind the counter must have sensed my anxiety because she finally asked me if she could be of assistance.

I told her that I was there to pick up Douglas.

She smiled and said, "One moment please."

I waited for about 20 more minutes but it seemed like a lot longer. I could feel my anxiety building as the minutes slowly moved around the clock on the wall. My palms were sweaty and my back was drenched.

This is what happens when you have PTSD—your mind defaults to panic mode the moment something doesn't go exactly as you expected it would. I managed to sit down on a bench right next to a cardboard box with a cat in it. The cat and I shared a moment of anxiety together. The cat was being taken to a new home, and I was worried that Douglas was no longer there.

Finally, a different lady came out and pulled me aside.

I just knew something was wrong and my level of anxiety was now in the stratosphere.

"Are you prepared to take Ace with you today?" she said.

"Yes, that is why I'm here," I answered in the most level tone of voice I could muster.

And then I paused and said, "Ace?"

I remembered then that I was the only one who knew Ace's new name, so I'd confused the front desk clerk when I'd said I was there to pick up "Douglas." All of this time while I'd been waiting in agony, she'd been searching high and low for a dog named Douglas. When she couldn't find one, she'd finally called her supervisor.

"Yes, Ace. Sorry," I quickly replied.

She walked me to the back to the cage where Douglas waited for me all clean and wearing a fresh red bandana around his neck. On the drive home Douglas was super-vigilant checking out everything that went by. He kept poking his head between the bucket seats of my Jeep as if to ask, "Are we there yet?" As we neared the house on the North Shore, my anxiety melted away.

* * *

I had bought all sorts of toys and a bed for Douglas as well as a Harley Davidson collar and chain. I'd also purchased a bone-shaped dog tag engraved with his name on it as well as contact numbers for both Sonja and I in case he ever got lost.

When Sonja got home, she was astounded to see just how big Douglas really was, now that he was home among all of our things.

"Geez!" she said. "We have adopted Clifford, the Big Red Dog!"

That first night, Douglas slept on the floor next to my side of the bed, apparently without a care in the world. The next morning, though, he began to pace. I could hear the clack of his toenails on the tile floor as he went from one end of our one-story beach house to the other as I lay in bed. When I got up, I also noticed he'd wet his bed. Not too bad for a first night of settling in, I thought to myself. Until I saw the rest of the house. His bed was not the only thing he'd marked while we slept—couches, pillows, and pretty much anything else he'd been able to reach, had been on the receiving end of his stream.

The adjustment period was about to begin. In the next few weeks Douglas would have to learn not to mark his territory. He would learn that I was the Alpha, and he needed to fall in line and be a good citizen.

* * *

As Douglas was learning how to be a good citizen under my tutelage, I was busy trying to convince my superiors that I wasn't a bad one. Although my life was finally starting to turnaround, I found myself in a bit of hot water when I was placed under investigation after being accused of having an extramarital affair with a woman I'd been romantically involved with prior to meeting Sonja.

In these cases, the Army will keep the person they are investigating completely in the dark and out of the loop, as they go about gathering the details of the case. So, as the accused, you are told what you are being investigated for, but you can't do anything to defend yourself while the investigation is underway, or you take the risk of being charged with obstruction.

As the investigation moved forward, the days and weeks moved slowly. I did nothing but sit at home and worry about the outcome. Every email or text notification would make my stomach twist in anticipation of receiving bad news, and every time the phone rang I jumped. Each day ended with discussing the events of the day with Sonja as they related to my case. There was not one minute when my thoughts were not consumed by this investigation. Forget about sleeping.

When the walls started to become too constrictive, Douglas and I would take walks up and down the beach to get some fresh air. Because it was the middle of the day, there'd be few other souls around. Douglas and I would sit quietly on the wet sand contemplating life, while we watched the magnificent 20-foot swells roll in. It was during these walks that I first began to notice that if I let out a sigh, Douglas would do the same. One night I asked Sonja if I sighed a lot. She confirmed that I did, adding it was especially noticeable when I was stressed. It seemed as though, in his own way, Douglas was taking on my pain and showing his empathy the only way he knew how—by mimicking my sounds of despair.

* * *

After three torturous months of being under investigation and living in a constant state of anxiety, stress and paranoia, I was feeling worn down and exhausted. I decided I would give up trying to fight the charges and accept whatever punishment they decided to give me. Guilty or not, I was ready to cry Uncle.

When I shared my thoughts with Sonja, she gave me a funny look.

"What are you talking about?" she said. "You've worked your ass off for 20 years of your life for the Army. You did something stupid, and you're ready to throw in the towel?"

She was a petite woman with a sweet disposition, but Lord help you if she got mad.

"I just don't have it in me to fight, and I really don't want to talk about this anymore," I said.

That night Sonja went on the Internet, researched similar cases and figured out how she could most effectively present my defense. She was up all night writing the rebuttal. There was no way she was going to stand by and watch me give up everything I'd worked so hard for (like I said before, she isn't a person you want angry at you!).

The next day I turned the paperwork in to my command for processing. It took about a week and I sat on pins and needles the entire time as I waited for the final decision. At this point I understood that the worst that could come out of it was that I would be reprimanded and have a black mark on my permanent record.

I still preferred to leave the Army with a clean record of conduct, having served honorably for most of my adult life. I had made far too many personal sacrifices for this to end up being my swan song. In the end, the general made his decision and I was able to complete my tour with no further incident.

The day I got the news that I'd been cleared, I arrived home to find Sonja and Douglas waiting for me. As I parked in the driveway and got out of my Jeep, Douglas pushed Sonja out of the way and came running out to me. Douglas has this way about him. When he's happy to see me, he manages to wag his entire body instead of just his tail and as he walks toward you he licks the air in anticipation of licking you.

As I was greeting Douglas, Sonja said, "So, how did it go?"

I kind of gave her that tight-upper-lip smile and responded with, "Well, it's over."

And we all walked into the house.

* * *

Douglas turned out to be a great friend and a treasured loved one in our home. It never really mattered what kind of day I had, Douglas was always happy to see me. This made me happy in return and allowed me the freedom to become comfortable with caring for another living being. Having Douglas also forced me to be more social. When we were out on our walks, we'd get stopped a lot, so I was forced to talk to more people. You just can't help but fall in love with Douglas once you've met him.

The more we bonded, the more I realized that interacting with Douglas was very therapeutic for me, so I decided to look for someone who specialized in training service dogs so I could continue working with him toward alleviating some of PTSD symptoms.

Douglas embarked on a three-month boot camp/behavior/ service dog training. Sometimes he'd be boarded for several weeks at the trainer's house and other times she'd come to our house to ensure we were using all the skills he was being taught, like how to wake me me up if he sensed I was having a nightmare or experiencing sleep apnea, or how to stand guard while accompanying me to an ATM (literally standing by and "watching my back").

Since then, I cannot tell you how many times I have been awakened by a heavy paw on my chest. At first I thought Douglas was just being a pain in the ass, but even if I locked him out of my bedroom, he would bark when he heard me snoring in order to wake me up. No matter what, Douglas wasn't going to stop until he no longer heard me snoring. His concern for me is genuine. I have truly been blessed with him.

* * *

Author's Note: please see back of the book for resources for PTSD dogs.

CHAPTER 14

LETTING GO

A PERSON MUCH WISER THAN I, used to say, "Life happens the way it is supposed to." I take that to mean that the experiences that ultimately shaped my life were all part of the great design. The trauma I experienced placed me in the right places at the right times to be able to save the lives of many of my fellow soldiers. This was apparently the journey I was destined for. It was never about me, it was about helping them. It was about the people I saved and those who I couldn't save, who I'll always mourn.

There is a difference between the changes brought on by life's natural progression and those brought about by surviving traumatic experiences. I am not talking about the credit card lines that appear from out of nowhere in the middle of your forehead as the years go by. I am talking about a seismic shift so powerful that it disrupts the very landscape of your destiny.

I can remember my life prior to developing PTSD—the version where my first spouse and I envisioned growing old together, while we watched our children grow up and have kids of their own. That life included the dream of living on a little ranch outside San Antonio, Texas, where there was plenty of room for family and friends and the living room walls were filled with family photos. In that version of my life, I was older but still basically the same, except wearing a white shirt and jeans rather than a military uniform.

Once upon a time, I'd envisioned this was what my life would become. But that was before PTSD derailed life's natural order.

Most of us change and evolve continuously over the course of a lifetime. It is this continuum of variations that shapes our personalities and determines our final outcome. I've often wondered how different my outcome would have been had I never enlisted in the Armed Forces.

Based on my beginnings, I would have been a man who worked in the hospitality industry, and there's a good chance that the ranch life I described above would have been a pretty accurate account of my story. I just smile now when I think about the dreams I had as a younger man, because they seem so irrelevant now.

PTSD is so much a part of what defines me as a human being today that I can't even imagine having never experienced it. This journey has made me who I am today—an altered version of myself that is stronger and wiser. I still miss the parts of my soul that are gone, but therapy has given me the tools to honor these changes rather than rail against them. I now see light where I once saw only darkness and have reclaimed my rightful place in society.

To that end, here's my advice to you: Let yourself come home. Relinquish the painful memories, guilt, sorrow, hopelessness, and fear you've been clinging to. Live in the moment. When you go to a restaurant, sit at a table facing your family instead of the business' entrance, and when you drive down the highway pay no attention to the debris on the side of the road. Pull your family in closer instead of pushing them away.

I am not saying any of this will happen overnight. For me, it was a slow progression filled with both small and great victories. Some of the more significant victories didn't even hit my radar until their magnitude was later pointed out to me.

One particular instance was when I celebrated St. Patrick's Day on the crowded streets of Hawaii's Chinatown in 2012 (If you want to find a great Irish bar in Hawaii, you go to Chinatown. Go figure!). There must have been hundreds of people walking around me in an ocean of green and I didn't even process that I was in the midst of a crowd until my wife leaned over and said, "You're doing pretty good."

That was a pretty big deal for somebody who historically would have walked two blocks out of the way to avoid walking down a crowded street. Before therapy, I never would have ventured into a street festival. I would have suffocated if I had. Being in a big crowd used to remind me too much of walking through congested marketplaces in war-torn countries where a kid could walk up and shove a grenade into your hand at any given moment. On that St.

Patrick's Day, however, I felt nothing noteworthy at all. I felt normal.

* * *

Letting go also means forgiving yourself. Forgiving myself was one of the best choices I have ever made in my life. Once I made that choice, I was able to start loving myself again.

I used to beat myself up over stuff that is either irrelevant or lands squarely in the "who-gives-a-shit?" category. At times, I did this to such an extent that I'd completely incapacitate myself. No matter how unrealistic or completely ridiculous my suspicions may have seemed to outsiders, for me it was reality.

For instance, I once turned in an insurance claim for damages to my motorcycle, and because it seemed to take longer than usual to hear back from the insurance company, I jumped to the conclusion that they'd decided to investigate me for a fraudulent claim. Of course it was a ridiculous conclusion to jump to. Everything was fine. I just panicked. Life is way too short to hold onto feelings of fear, paranoia, guilt and panic.

* * *

I will never be able to say that I am completely healed of PTSD. It becomes part of your personality and who you are. The person I see in the mirror today is certainly not the same one who was there years ago. That person is long gone. But, you can't pound a square peg into a round hole, and I've wasted too many years trying to do just that. Sure, I've been permanently derailed from the path I'd once been on, but I've also had the opportunity to grow stronger and smarter.

I still have nightmares, typically triggered by something I see on TV. I once made the mistake of watching the movie "The Hurt Locker" and lay awake tossing and turning and thinking about those scenes for days afterward. There is not a movie in the world that can recreate the shit I've seen, but some come pretty close and that's frightening. Douglas still stands watch over me every night and is quick to drop a paw on my face or lick me with his "I just licked my asshole breath" any time this happens.

Big crowds no longer bother me as much as they used to and I can sit anywhere I want in any restaurant. The anger within is no longer there. The feeling of guilt is subsiding, because I choose not to give into those feelings, and every day I notice something else I'd never noticed before.

Where I used to see only gray skies I now see beauty: a cool ocean breeze, the aroma of plumeria blooming or the sound of my own laughter filled with joy where it was once tinged with sarcasm and defiance. A few years ago I saw a picture of myself and I was smiling not only with my mouth but also with my eyes. I was clearly in a happy moment. I hadn't seen myself that way in so long, I almost didn't recognize the expression. I actually did a double take.

I used to sometimes wonder what my life would have been like had I never joined the military. But for all of its ups and downs, enlisting gave me the opportunity to see things that most people only read about. I have met extraordinary people, and traveled to extraordinary places all over the world. Good, bad or indifferent, it has been a great ride, and I now find great satisfaction in giving back to our veteran community through my motorcycle club (Warrior Brotherhood) or through Healing Wounds, the nonprofit organization Sonja and I have founded to help those affected by PTSD.

Any day that I can help out a Veteran in need is a good day.

I also spend every day being thankful for my new life and I look forward to the man I am becoming—a kinder, more patient father and husband. A gentler soul.

I have been granted the ultimate do-over and people don't get do-overs very often.

If you are ever granted the same opportunity, do it right and do it well.

You won't regret it.

AS IT IS TYPICAL WITH a closure of a chapter everyone wants to know what happened to some of the people I talked about in the book.

Sonja and I had a beautiful baby boy and he takes up a lot of our time. My son Marco lives with us and goes to college full time. He loves his baby brother and is teaching him great things. We continue work at healing my own wounds and serving veterans in my area. Sonja is in private practice specializing in trauma treatment and both of us are heavily involved with our non-profit work through healing wounds. We do yearly fundraisers aimed towards increased awareness for PTSD and at helping vets connect with good resources we provide at www.HealingsWounds.org.

Both my adult daughters are not speaking to me secondary to my Divorce with their mother. I hope that one day they can understand that I will always be their father and my love for them is unconditional.

Sam, David and Lance are still very good friends and we talk often on social media. Morris my guide in Africa is also on social media, and every once in a while he will like one of my posts.

Douglas spends his days lying in the healing sun and at night he sleeps vigilantly by my side ready to wake me up when I have nightmares.

ABOUT THE AUTHOR

MARC RACITI

MARC C. RACITI ENLISTED INTO the Army in 1989 as a clerk typist (71L). Shortly after completing basic training and advanced individual training, he deployed to Bahrain, in support of Operation Desert Storm with the 47th Field Hospital. It was there he fell in love with medicine and decided to pursue a career as a Physician Assistant (PA).

In 1997 he graduated from the University of Texas Health Science Center in San Antonio and was commissioned to second lieutenant. In 2001 he completed his Fellowship in Orthopedics through Womack Army Community Hospital. Marc spent the rest of his army career treating, and caring for the sick and wounded.

He deployed four more times, twice to Iraq, the Balkans and to Africa; frequently provided good medicine in bad places. In 2013, after 24 years of service, he retired from the Army as a Major. His last assignment was to Hawaii where he met his current wife Sonja.

Marc presently lives in Scottsdale, Arizona with Sonja and his adult son Marco and baby Makana. He continues riding his motorcycle with a veteran MC, working as an orthopedic PA and is very active in the veteran community. Sonja is a civilian as well and has opened up a private practice specializing in PTSD treatment. Douglas, his service dog, is happy living out his days basking in the Arizona sun and gobbling down any and all treats.

RESOURCES

There are plenty of veteran groups out there who are interested in helping out as well. Here are a few of my favorite ones:

IRAQI/AFGHANISTAN VETERANS OF AMERICA:

http://iava.org/#

IAVA provides valuable resources and empowers veterans to connect with one another, fostering a strong and lasting community. Through education, advocacy and community building, we strive to create a country which honors and supports veterans of all generations.

PARALYZED VETERANS OF AMERICA:

http://www.pva.org/site/c.ajIRK9NJLcJ2E/b.6305401/k. BCBB/Home.htm

Paralyzed Veterans of America, a congressionally chartered veterans service organization founded in 1946, has developed a unique expertise on a wide variety of issues involving the special needs of our members – veterans of the armed forces who have experienced spinal cord injury or dysfunction.

STUDENTS VETERAN OF AMERICA:

http://www.studentveterans.org

Since SVA's founding in 2008, over one million veterans have returned home to pursue a postsecondary degree or certificate using VA educational benefits. To meet this need, SVA's presence at the local and national levels has grown to include over 1,300 chapter affiliates, numerous private and nonprofit partners, and most importantly, an expanding list of impactful programs and services for veterans.

The nation's renewed focus on veteran welfare has ignited change on campuses and in congress. SVA is committed to capitalizing on this momentum to ensure today's and tomorrow's veterans are supported in their transition to education and employment.

There are many resources for help both in the military and in the civilian sector. There are several non-profit organizations that focus on PTSD and helping people return to their life.

MILITARYWITHPTSD.ORG:

http://www.militarywithptsd.org

The Strength of a Warrior program features a variety of training exercises designed to help veterans overcome personal challenges as they integrate back into civilian life. Some of what Strength of a Warrior offers is: education about Post Traumatic Stress Disorder (PTSD), a self-check questioner for PTSD, online self help worksheets, and resources for veterans.

PTSDUNITED.ORG:

http://www.ptsdunited.org/about/what-is-ptsd-united

PTSD United, Inc. is a 501(c)3 non-profit organization dedicated to providing support and resources for sufferers of PTSD, their families and caregivers, and anyone interested in learning more about Post Traumatic Stress. Among our growing areas of focus, our flagship program is huddl.org: the Anonymous Support Network for Trauma. Huddl.org is a free, completely anonymous online community available twenty-four hours a day, seven days a week where people can go to connect with others living with PTSD

SERVICE DOGS:

Any Veteran officially diagnosed with PTSD can request a PTSD service dog. There are several organizations that will work with you and your dog so that you are both properly trained. Some organizations will provide you with a PTSD dog if you are accepted into their program - it costs about 20-25K to train a dog. Training does take a lot of time and energy, but the payoff is great. Here is Douglas, Marc's PTSD dog. The links below will get you started with more information.

http://www.servicedogsforamerica.org/apply/ptsd-service-dog/

http://www.pawsforveterans.com

http://www.patriotpaws.org/ http://www.sheltertosoldier.org http://www.petsforvets.com

http://www.thisableveteran.org

http://www.brotherandsisterptsddogs.org http://www.k9sforwarriors.org

DOUGLAS WITH HIS PTSD VEST LOOKING HANDSOME

SELF HELP NUMBERS:

Suicidal:

* National Suicide Prevention Lifeline: 1 (800) 273-8255

* Veterans Crisis Line : 1 (800) 273-8255 and Press 1
    Don't want to talk? You can text Text "GO" to 741-741

* Veteran Combat Call Center: 1 (800) 927-8387

Finding an off base therapist:

* http://www.MilitaryOneSource.mil   (1-800-342-9647) helps find counselors who are able to do face-to-face, online, telephonic and via video short-term treatment (12 sessions or less) at no cost. Available for family members as well.

* www.giveanhour.org - Therapist donate their services at no cost to military and loved ones (including friends, boyfriends, roommates and more)

* http://intransition.dcoe.mil/ In Transition (1-800-424-7877) is a program if you are PCSing and/or if you are transitioning into civilian life. They help with finding resources in your new area and help set up appointments for you. They can also assist with finding a place to live if needed and getting connected with the local VA.

* http://purplestarveterans.org: help with finding peer mentors in your area.

Cutting/Self Injurious Behavior

* Safe Alternatives, www.selfinjury.com; Email SAFE Alternatives at info@selfinjury.com or call 1-800-366-8288 for information on seeking help

Dating Abuse & Domestic Violence

* National Domestic Violence Hotline; www.thehotline.org 1-800-799-7233 (24/7) or TTY 1-800-787-3224

* RAINN: Rape, Abuse and Incest National Network; 1-800-656-4673 (24/7); www.rainn.org: 'Live Chat with RAINN (24/7)

Wilderness trip with other vets

*   Outward bound: www.outwardbound.org helps thousands of returning service members and recent veterans readjust to life at home through powerful wilderness courses that draw on the healing benefit of teamwork and challenge through use of the natural world.

WWW.HEALINGWOUNDS.ORG

Made in the USA
Middletown, DE
02 September 2017